MASTER YOUR THOUGHTS
MASTER YOUR LIFE

Bhupendra Singh Rathore

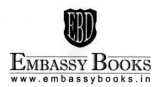

EMBASSY BOOKS
www.embassybooks.in

MASTER YOUR THOUGHTS MASTER YOUR LIFE
© Bhupendra Singh Rathore 2016

First Edition 2016

Published in India by:
Embassy Book Distributors
120, Great Western Building,
Maharashtra Chamber of Commerce Lane,
Fort, Mumbai 400 023, India
Tel: (+9122) -30967415, 22819546
Email: info@embassybooks.in
www.embassybooks.in

ISBN: 978-93-85492-81-5

Layout and typesetting by PSV Kumarasamy

Printed & Bound in India by Repro India Ltd., Navi Mumbai

Contents

Introduction

Situation 1:

> *Tring-tring!*
>
> *"Hey Ritu! What a coincidence - I was just thinking about you!"*

Situation 2:

> *"Sheesh! I had this weird feeling that I would lose my purse today. I don't know why. I just saw it coming... and I actually did lose it!"*

Almost everyone's been in scenarios like these, and probably more than once. They are so common that no one is surprised when they do happen.

Such incidents have become a part of our daily lives. We have accepted them as a natural phenomenon. How many of us have asked this question, "Why do such things happen?" Although most of us dismiss such situations as 'coincidence' or 'bad luck,' they have usually never given it more thought than that. But what if these incidents are not accidents or dumb luck, but have actually been brought into our lives by our own thoughts?

Welcome to the most powerful world of all - that of your mind!

- A one-year-old baby miraculously survived a bus accident where all the other passengers died.

- A patient given thirty days to live manages to lead a healthy life for another thirty years.

- Your end-of-term examination has just finished. You had only studied about a quarter of the syllabus, but most of the questions appear from what you read.

Many such incidents take place all over the world and neither science nor scientists can explain them. Are these not miracles? Miracles *do* happen. They happen for those who are focused, enthusiastic, filled with positive energy, and who give their best and always think big. I would say that a miracle is something that makes something impossible possible. For me, a miracle is something that you dream of but don't work for, and yet becomes a reality - just like magic!

The best part is that God has gifted us with the amazing power of creating magic. This may seem esoteric to a person who doesn't understand what magic is, but ask a magician and he will tell you how it works. And there is perfect logic to it - careful planning, precise timing, and a valid scientific explanation... right? Unfortunately, most of us observe our own lives as spectators despite having the power to be a magician.

So read on and we will break through some of these self-made barriers constraining our mind - after we say the magical word. No, it's not 'abracadabra.' It's *tathastu*.

Tathastu is a Sanskrit word that loosely translates as 'so be it' or 'your wish is granted.' But who says *tathastu*? Who makes all our wishes come true? The answer to both these questions is very simple - the secret lies within our own mind!

You must have heard of the great sages and monks who walked through fire and on water. The dark, lonely depths of the Himalayas are still said to be the home of sages who have been meditating there for decades without food and water, defying even death! Then there are those amazing stories of men pulling trains with their teeth, holding their breath while a truck runs over their chests, and bending iron rods with their eyes! In the past, science dismissed all these as nonsense. But today, science acknowledges that such miracles do happen, and they have supported them with relevant scientific proof. Quantum physics is a stream of study that is delving into the enormous power of the mind and is making progress in leaps and bounds.

Physics tells us that the entire Universe is a huge magnet with a vast magnetic field. We are powerhouses of magnetic bodies. What we think, say, dream, and desire has a magnetic strength that connects us with the greater magnetic wavelength of the Universe. This magnetic strength has signals that contain electrons, protons, and neutrons, which, though invisible to the naked eye, can be viewed under a powerful microscope. They exist even though we cannot see them. We release these entities into the atmosphere. Then they vibrate with the combined energy of the electrons, protons, and neutrons of the same wavelength of the Universe and bring home the wish, materializing the thought.

So this means that the signals of a good thought will attract and combine with a similar wavelength of the Universe, while a bad thought will attract and combine with its corresponding wavelength. And both will bring home the results of their individual thoughts. Our Universe has the magical force that can give you anything you want. Happiness, health, wealth - anything! It's the natural law of the Universe. It is the Law of Attraction. This law can be summarized in a few points:

- Believe in yourself, as you are a part of God, and God is nothing but you
- Do what you love to do and always be joyful
- Take massive Leaps of Faiths

The Law of Attraction is always in full force even

when we are asleep and not consciously aware of it. Through one of my most powerful workshops, called *Igniting the Spark*, I have tried to reach out to as many people as I possibly can, to make them aware of the Law of Attraction and the power of the mind through which this law works. There are step-by-step methods on how to use this law and there is a scientific explanation as to how the law works. This book will help you understand the inner working of your most powerful asset - your mind - so that you can utilize it to its fullest.

It has been an interesting journey for me since the time I decided to become a motivational speaker and corporate trainer. This has provided meaning and direction to my life when I decided to go through this learning myself. There was a point of time in my life when I was not sure what my future would be like. I was directionless. I didn't really know what I wanted to do in life. I wanted to achieve something, obviously, but I didn't know exactly what that 'something' was. My mind was a junkyard of meaningless thoughts, and I could not sift through them effectively.

Since I had decided that I didn't want to be conventional, I was labeled as incompetent, useless, directionless, as someone who would not succeed in life. I took all those labels seriously, and did not believe in myself. I stumbled. Whenever I saw someone who was more successful than I was, I was uncomfortable. I saw them as highly superior being and thought that it would be impossible for me to be like them. At that time, I was not aware of the things I knew, but what I didn't know that I can be explore books and get myself acquainted.

I was averse to doing anything with the remotest chance of failure. I was terrified of failing. Even at school and college I never participated in any competition. I took the easy way out. Today, when I look back, I realize that had I continued to take the easy way out, I would have been responsible for the murder of my real self.

There were some things that I really wanted to do, but thanks to my mindset, every time I attempted anything I would always fail. To me, it was always someone else's fault - never mine. And then there were those two big words that we all take refuge in from time to time - 'luck' and 'fate.'

When I started my training, it was initially to improve my English. Then in a seemingly muddled chain of events, one thing automatically led to another until I reached my zenith. I was made to realize, through these sessions and by my guru, that everything that we are searching for lies within us, in our subconscious mind. No outside force is responsible for our achievements, our emotions, and our morals. The responsibility lies with us. One of my gurus put it very aptly: "All you need lies within you now."

And after going through many practical life

experiences, I can assure you, with great confidence, that all you really need is indeed within you. And I'm sure that by the time you finish this book, you will also start believing it.

This knowledge changed my life, gave me the direction I needed, and provided me with the burning desire to share it. I wanted to reach out to as many people as I possibly could and share with them the logic behind the magic. And now you, dear reader, have this knowledge in front of you, so let's dive in!

1

Laws of the Mind

I'm sure many of you have come across a situation where, say, you had a hunch about something and it turned out to be true, or you didn't want someone to do something and he did just that.

We often wonder just how we knew that or why such a thing happened, but the answer is both simple and complex. Simple because it is related to our own mind; and complex because it involves understanding the way our mind functions and how we attract most of the things in our lives. If you can master your mind, you can master your life. As Buddha had said, "The mind is everything. What you think you become."

Here's a simple analogy. Mr. Sharma, a businessman, goes to a restaurant with his clients. He orders the chicken special, and after placing the order he becomes engrossed in a discussion with his clients. Twenty minutes later, the waiter comes and serves them their dishes, placing the chicken special in front of Mr. Sharma.

Mr. Sharma says, "Excuse me, waiter, but I never ordered this dish."

Confused, the waiter checks his pad and replies, "I'm sorry, sir, but this *is* the dish you ordered. I have it written here."

Mr. Sharma vehemently responds, "Do you think I'm a fool? I didn't order the chicken special. I ordered something else."

The waiter, startled at this behavior, tentatively suggests that perhaps he forgot what he had ordered. Mr. Sharma is enraged, and the conversation turns into a full-blown argument.

The actual problem here is that Mr. Sharma suffers from short-term memory loss, a medical condition, and hence he had forgotten what he had ordered. And on top of this, he isn't even aware that he has the condition.

Similarly, we are all seated in the gigantic restaurant that is the Universe and we are constantly ordering something from its endless catalog. We order not only by asking, but also by feeling, thinking, speaking, and acting. At this very moment, your feelings are what dictate your order, and that is what you will receive. But like Mr. Sharma, we also we suffer from real-time memory loss.

By the time our order has been processed and delivered to us, we tend to forget what we had ordered, and then we say, "Hey, I didn't order this." We do not take into account our thoughts and feelings because we fail to comprehend their power.

Every restaurant has one rule - you can change your order, but only if they have not started preparing it already. In the same way, you can cancel the order you have placed in the Universe if you are aware of what you are ordering, because the best part about the Universe is that nothing happens instantly. It takes time for the order to be processed.

To understand how to order something from the catalog of the Universe, it is important to understand the laws of our own mind. These laws bind us with the Universe. The first time I heard about the laws of the mind, I wondered, "If the mind is supposed to be boundless and infinite, then how would it strictly follow a law?"

Here are a few characteristics of the mind.

1. The mind does not understand words or language. It only comprehends images.

That's why we remember things better when we see them. If I were to say a phrase to you, I'm sure you will picture it in your mind. Let's test it out.

"A person is carrying a red bag on his shoulder."

Well, what happened? Did you read what I had written or did you imagine a person carrying a red bag on his shoulder?

That's what your mind does. If you tell yourself, "I don't want debts, I don't want negativity, I don't want problems," it just visualizes more debts, negativity, and problems! You are constantly ordering what your mind is visualizing and what your heart is feeling.

Be careful! If you have any negative or pessimistic feelings, you need to dismiss them immediately, or you will fall into the trap of this law. Take powerful action - sing loudly, dance vibrantly, listen to some uplifting music - do whatever you want to do, but *do* something.

All great leaders only focus on what they want, not what they don't want, and that's one of the biggest secrets to their success. Do you want to be the next success story? If so, then take charge.

2. The mind doesn't understand the difference between imagination and reality.

That's why we cry when we watch a sad movie or horror movie terrifies us for days afterwards even though we tell ourselves over and over that it was only a movie.

Fear is created when you visualize something that has not happened or did happen in the past, but you don't want it to happen again. Fear paralyzes you because it's difficult for your subconscious mind to distinguish between imagination and reality. When you are scared, your mind is filled with negative thoughts. The origins of these thoughts could be a film, an incident that happened in the past, or just plain old imagination. Even though we know that our fear is irrational, we react to it as if it is actually happening.

How many of us feel that we're on the verge of a nervous breakdown before an important examination? Many of us, because the thought of a probable failure paralyzes us and drives us crazy!

Some time ago, a house caught fire. A happy family of four lived in that house. When the fire broke out, the mother and the two kids were asleep as it was late at night. The mother somehow found the courage to evacuate her children, but could not save herself. She screamed at the top of her lungs for help. People rushed to save her, but the fire was out of control. By the time fire brigade arrived, the lady had suffered severe burns and died. It was indeed a horrible scene.

This would be a saddening story - if it were true. Wake up! Whatever I have just told you is a lie. But without thinking whether it was true or false, your mind immediately visualized the entire scene. I am sure you must have imagined the house on fire, the lady struggling to save her kids, screaming for help, and eventually dying. That's what your mind does. Now read this story:

Imagine that there are 5,000 people seated in an auditorium. They have come to hear you speak - you are one of the top speakers in the country. You are a person who has helped transform millions of lives. A person goes on stage and introduces you in glowing terms, and the moment you appear on stage, the entire audience greets you with a standing ovation. You look around and all you can see is people standing up and applauding you. The sounds of those claps fill you with great joy and excitement. Once the audience sits down, you begin to share your wisdom with them. They listen with deep concentration; your words make them sit still on the edge of their seats. In the first row of the auditorium you can see your parents, brother, sister, spouse, children, close friends, and relatives. Whenever you glance at them, you can see them smiling proudly at hearing you speak with such confidence and charm. And when the speech is over, there's another thundering round of applause from the audience. The sight of your success brings tears to your parents' eyes. They come on stage and give you a warm hug in front of the huge crowd, and when they step away, there's a long queue of people waiting eagerly to get your autograph.

WOW! Now isn't that a powerful image? This time, I'm sure you can literally see yourself standing in front of 5,000 people, hearing them clap, and receiving warm hugs from your family and friends. You must have felt great after reading it.

What I wanted to convey to you in these two stories was that your mind is a brilliant connection-making machine. The moment you have a thought, the mind connects the dots, processes them, and then starts to produce images that look real. The pictures are created so well that the mind itself can't distinguish between what is real and what is not.

Your mind is a great servant. If you make it see the right picture, it will always fire the right signals for your body to act and ultimately you will achieve what you want. That's why it is said that whatever you create in your mind, it will always be achieved. That's the reason why visualization plays such an important role in your success.

Visualize what you want to happen and then see the miraculous way in which things unfold.

3. The mind likes doing the least work possible.

We always search for the easy way out. This brings us to the theory of how to calculate pain and pleasure, which will be discussed later in the book.

How many times have you promised yourself to get up early in the morning, but when the alarm rings you keep hitting the snooze button so that by the time you get up, it's very late? Or think about the time when someone forced you to study or when you forced yourself to study - and compare the productivity with what you achieved when you actually felt like studying and did it by yourself. It would be a lot higher.

Ever wondered why such things happen?

They happen because your mind doesn't really want to work hard. The mind is like a stubborn child. As a result, we can't really force it to perform. All we can do is bribe or manipulate it sometimes.

Have you ever noticed that sometimes when you are engrossed in something you tend to lose track of time and forget about being hungry and other mundane matters? This is the time when you work tirelessly and feel great about it, too. When you concentrate on what you are passionate about, you do your best work. This is because if your mind likes doing something, it will not get tired or perceive it as forced or hard labor. It will cooperate because it loves what you are doing.

If you don't like your job and have no option but to stick to it, then my suggestion to you is this: don't push yourself to perform. The more you push, the more tired you get, and then you may begin to lose hope. Instead, start visualizing the best possible outcome. Try to be more creative in your work. After every hour, do something positive that will excite and energize you. This can be as simple as talking to a close friend or reading a page of a graphic novel. And be grateful for what you have - there are many who have far less than you. Appreciate yourself. Soon you will begin to notice that the job that you initially didn't like is beginning to seem less painful, and that your mind is finding ways to get aligned with it or is helping you find something that excites you.

The rule of thumb is that if you force your mind, you will receive something that you will never appreciate or respect, simply because your mind perceives it be an effort and hence will resist it.

4. The mind acts faster on others' commands.

This has proved to be true time and again. We refuse to listen to ourselves easily. Often our mind doesn't accept the commands we feed it, but it always accepts and reacts to the commands others provide. This is the reason why we learn faster when people teach us rather than when we read and understand for ourselves.

According to Hindu mythology, Lord Hanuman was one of the most powerful deities of all. His powers were boundless. As a child, he had taken a giant leap and grabbed the Sun with his mouth, mistaking it for a fruit. He could destroy anyone or anything with just one powerful punch. But when he grew up, he was cursed to forget all about his powers. When Lord Rama wanted to send a message to warn Ravana and to locate Sita, he discovered that he had no one who could jump across the ocean. Then Jamwant reminded Lord Hanuman about his powers and his childhood adventures. The moment Lord Hanuman remembered his powers, he stood up and bounded across the ocean with one leap and killed many devils like Sursa, Sinhini, Lankini, and Akshaykumar.

We all need a Jamwant in our lives, who can remind us about our own powers since we are powerful beyond measure. That's probably the reason why important CEOs, leaders, and athletes have personal trainers who guide them, motivate them, and remind them about their strengths.

Unfortunately, the reverse also holds true. When we are told about our weaknesses and faults or are criticized, the mind acts on these commands as well. That's why when I am asked how a person can remain positive throughout one's life, I suggest, "Surround yourself with positive people and stay away from negative people as much as possible."

5. Whatever the human mind can conceive, it can achieve.

This is the ultimate truth! Your mind is like a powerful magnet that has the power to attract whatever it wants.

If you leave your home to go to New Delhi, you will reach New Delhi, not New York. You will only reach New York when you decide to go there.

Wherever you have reached or whatever you have achieved depended on what you thought and how you acted upon your thoughts.

If you listen around, you will often hear people talking about earning handsome salaries one day - salaries between thirty thousand and a lakh. Most of them do eventually achieve the goal they have dreamed of, but only after much hard work and effort. Then there are the people who dream about earning crores and leading a luxurious lifestyle. They, too, eventually get what they dreamed of.

One of the laws of life is that if you think about something repeatedly and with great intensity, the mind, after a point of time, starts to believe in it and does everything possible to turn it into a reality.

I often ask people why they don't think big. The truth is that regardless of big or small, you use up the same amount of energy. However, negative thoughts consume greater energy than positive thoughts. And that is what has given rise to the phrase "think big!" There is definitely some logic behind it.

6. The mind craves balance.

The law of conservation of energy says that energy can never be created or destroyed. The Universe will always have the same energy as it had on the day of its creation. Your very existence is a natural process and your subconscious mind works in sync with that process. It never goes out of sync. If your conscious mind disturbs this delicate balance, then your subconscious mind will do everything possible to bring it back.

Your mind will never accept this imbalance. Take a look at life and the world around you and you will see that balance is all around you - positive and negative, right and wrong, good and evil, day and night. It's all about harmony. Your mind does whatever it can to restore balance.

7. The mind is powerful beyond measure.

It is said that no one can understand just how powerful our mind is. Even exceedingly smart people like Einstein or Newton did not use more than five percent of their brains. If that is so, how much of our brains do we use? Yes, your brain can make you achieve almost anything you want. Its power is immeasurable. When we compare one person with another, the comparisons are usually based on their achievements, since that's all that we can see. But how can we measure the power of our own minds? To do so, we must attempt to push our limits - to take the so-called leap of faith. This is achieved by taking positive risks, by trusting ourselves, and believing that we can do it.

All I can say at this time is that if you can fine-tune your mind and energy to any task in this world, then you will definitely reach where you want to go.

Knowing all these laws of the mind makes you realize that if you really want to reach your goal, then show your mind the right picture. Don't push yourself. Instead, be passionate about what you want to achieve. Only then will you see the speed with which your life changes.

Thoughts are converted into things and provided to you even if you don't know how it works. Have absolute faith, for only then will you definitely get what you want.

A few days ago, I received a call from a lady. She said that she after reading my book and watching the video, she "just had to talk to me." She asked me very politely if I had some time because she wanted to narrate her story to me. I was curious, and listened. This is her story:

She comes from a small but very beautiful hill station in India called Shillong. Shillong is the capital of Meghalaya, and is situated in the north-eastern part of the country.

Shillong is often referred to as the "Scotland of the East." When she first learnt this, she was just twelve years old. Since then, she had developed a yearning to visit Scotland. She spent hours on end searching for books and magazines so that she could learn more about the place, to see pictures that would show her what the country and its people looked like. She read about its history and its celebrated monuments. The amount of readily available material on Scotland surprised her, whether it was an article in the newspaper, travel brochures promoting it as a great honeymoon destination, or reports of a sudden record snowfall that disrupted normal life. A few days later, an old school friend mentioned that a cousin was coming to Shillong to visit the family, and guess what? He was from Scotland!

Then the school announced a farewell party for a teacher who was leaving to get married - and was going to live in Scotland! "How strange," she thought, "why am I hearing so much about Scotland all of a sudden?"

A few days later, she heard her brother-in-law and his friends discussing the Scottish way of speaking English and how different it was from the rest of Britain. It almost felt as if she had been virtually transported to Scotland.

But with the passage of time, she forgot about her desire to visit Scotland, though whenever anyone remarked, "Oh, Shillong? Isn't that a hill station? I've heard it's very beautiful," she would invariably swell with pride and reply, "Yes, it's very beautiful. It's also known as the Scotland of the East."

Later, when it was time for her to get married, she received many proposals, and a good number of marriage prospects were from Scotland. Although none of them materialized, they rekindled her desire to visit the land of her dreams. Eventually, she moved to Delhi and got married. A week after the marriage, her husband announced that their honeymoon destination was - you guessed it, Scotland!

This impossible dream of a schoolgirl living in a remote corner of India about a faraway country actually became a reality. She had dared to dream big, had communicated this dream to the Universe, and her wish was granted. The Universe had said *tathastu*. Her other dreams - of buying a cute little red car with her own hard-earned money, and of marrying the man of her choice - also came true. As a little girl, she didn't know what restraint meant, and so she dreamed her wildest dreams.

If you read her story carefully, you will realize that she had unknowingly followed all the laws of the mind. This is what we all do. We follow all the laws of the Universe since there is no other way of living. But unfortunately, most of us are unaware of those laws.

I had a strong desire to make a difference to the lives of others, but when I wanted to follow my heart I did not know how to do so. So I left my job and started a company called BSR Sparssh Foundation. My challenge was that I had no real experience of running companies or of being an entrepreneur. I hired a few people, but I didn't know how to utilize them well. I had people whom I knew were capable of working, but I couldn't keep them engaged. Eventually a point came when I had to ask them to leave or they themselves left.

I had people who could have delivered, and I did

my best with them even though my experience at that time was limited. But I still landed up in a situation that exhausted me. It was my ignorance that placed me in that situation. Had I known how to keep them engaged, I am sure the situation would have been different.

Most people don't know that they can really learn and remember facts at the speed of a computer. They still use their memory power to store the information the way they want to. I was also one of them until I met a person who could learn a hundred words in less than five minutes and recall them perfectly. Five minutes later, he could tell me all the words in reverse. I was surprised and asked him how he did it. He replied, "You can learn it, too. It won't take more than three days." I did learn it and I realized that I could do the same. I was unaware of the power of my own memory, but the moment I became aware of it, I started using it in a much better way. I can also teach this art to you in just twenty-four hours.

It's not a rocket science, but it will give you an insight into what your mind can achieve if you put your heart into it.

You, too, have unlimited powers right now - in the form of your mind. But if you want better results, you have to learn how to harness that power. Most people use that power, but not in the right way. I'm sure you would love to get the best out of your life, so I'll reveal some of the secrets on how to reach your ultimate destination.

The Universe says your wish is my command. Each time you make a wish it says *tathastu*. Each time you feel a certain way, it says, "I will give you more of that feeling." Every time you say something, that's what it takes as its command. It has no brain of its own. It just works. It doesn't have the ability to distinguish between what is good or bad or what is right or wrong.

It is often said that if we refuse to accept anything but the best, then we will usually get the best.

So what exactly is mind power, the Law of Attraction and universal power? How do they work? Are these just thoughts to motivate us or is there some substance to them?

The whole world is a magnet. Our Universe is a huge ball of energy. This is not something I'm making up, it's pure science. If you look at an eighth-standard physics textbook you will discover that everything in the Universe can be broken down into their component elements. Each element can be then broken down into its atoms, which have protons, neutrons, and electrons in different combinations that dictate the character of that element. Physics will tell you that all these protons, neutrons, and electrons are never at rest. They are governed by the Law of Attraction. Protons and electrons are attracted to each other because protons are positive and electrons are negative. Neutrons are neutral. They are constantly vibrating within a set position with a certain energy. When this energy is challenged due to proximity to some other element with a stronger magnetic field that can change their combination and attract protons, neutrons, and electrons, they change form. They combine into something else.

Science will tell you that nothing in this world can be created or destroyed. The form may change, but they always exist. Water, when subjected to heat, becomes a vapor. When frozen, it becomes ice. All three have distinctly different characteristics but come from the same elements—a combination of hydrogen and oxygen.

Everything works with one infinite power. Everything in this Universe, from a speck of dust to a human being, is a powerhouse of energy. We are governed by one law - the Law of Attraction. And we humans are the most powerful magnets in the Universe. When we think, we emit unfathomable magnetic signals into the Universe. The stronger our thoughts, the stronger are the signals that we are sending to the Universe. If we think about money, we knowingly or unknowingly attract everything that has to do with money. For example, if you are determined the make more money you will automatically attract opportunities that will yield money. On the other hand, if your thoughts are clouded with fear - the fear of losing money, say by being robbed - then that's exactly what will happen to you. By thinking about money, you will draw more money towards you, but if your thoughts are negative then this will probably result in you losing money.

The Universe obeys the Law of Attraction as it receives the signals and converts them into the desired combinations. No signals are lost. No powerful thoughts have ever been disobeyed. No wish has been left unfulfilled. No desire has been left incomplete.

The Universe knows just one thing: how to give you what you ask for.

The law does not operate with any logic or reasoning. It just says that I will give you everything you want. If a person jumps from a tall building, they will die, irrespective of whether that person was good or bad. That is how the Law of Attraction works. You ask, the Universe delivers. This is the law that governs the entire Universe.

You just need to be aware of it at all times and consciously apply it to your daily life. The Universe has no quota in its granary, there is abundance for each and every person on Earth - there are simply no limitations. The only condition is to make a wish - as big as you like - and believe in it with all your heart. Let it take root in your consciousness. Go to sleep with it on your mind, because even when we are asleep our subconscious mind is at work and keeps sending powerful signals to the Universe. It's extremely important to set free the greatest wish of our life and see the magic of our own mind come to play.

There are three major beliefs that govern the way we live, and these are the reasons why some people are content and others discontent. These underlying beliefs are:

1. *Belief that there is a lack of what they want.*

2. *Belief that there is enough of what they want.*

3. *Belief that there is more than enough of what they want.*

Let me explain what these are and the role that they play in a person's life. Let's start with the first one.

1. Belief that there is a lack of what they want.

People who belong to this group are people who have limited thoughts. They believe that there is a lack of everything. Even their dreams are small because they have some inbuilt notion that dreams signify greed, and that someone who is greedy is a bad person. They also believe that if they dream or hope for too much, their wishes will never be fulfilled. The fear factor always dominates, and as a result they begin to doubt their abilities. They don't believe that they can do it.

You ask them, "What about the person next to you who has done it?"

They would reply, "He is different. I am a simple man. I don't have the good fortune to be like him. Everyone is not so lucky to have everything in life." This way of thinking is an example of lack mentality.

I meet many people who tell me, "I will be very happy when I achieve my goal." And when I ask them if they are happy right now, they say, "I'm not sure, but when I reach my destination I will undoubtedly be happy." Wow! What an ironic notion - how can you be sad when you are creating your own life and shaping your destiny?

Let me warn you, if you remain sad, the message being sent to the Universe says that you are operating from a belief that says, "There is a lack in my life." And if you have understood what I have been saying so far, then you will also understand that the Universe only responds to your feelings and thoughts. If you doubt the Universe and are uncertain, you will remain unhappy, sad, and low!

This very belief is the difference between the 80 percent who keep struggling to turn their dreams into reality and the 20 percent who have realized most of their dreams.

If you want to create magic in your life, then you must learn to get rid of these limiting thought processes and start believing that the Universe has enough for everyone. There is no lack in the Universe. Every 'lack' is in your mind. Every obstacle is created by you.

A great example is an episode from my own life. I was born in a village called Khatoli, situated in Rajasthan's Ajmer district. I came from an ordinary family. My father was a farmer and life was very difficult as there was never enough for all of us. However, my father always ensured that there was enough money for our education.

A sweetened, colored block of ice cost 50 paisa. It was sold by a disheveled sixty-year-old man on a street corner. For us as kids, this treat was the epitome of luxury, and the best part of it was that we could afford to buy it.

As I grew up, my father managed to arrange funds so that I could complete my course in computers from NIIT. I was good at it, but my biggest challenge was that my spoken English was restricted to a few words and phrases. To string a complete sentence together was a very difficult task. When I had to deliver my first presentation in English—at the institute, it was a disaster! I walked onto the stage but just stammered and said nothing. It was then that I knew I had to do something about it. A few weeks later, there was a get-together in the institute where we were all asked some fun questions. The question I was asked was how would I convince my parents if I wanted to marry a woman who was seven years older than me. The question was in English! And I didn't know what the word 'convince' meant. All I could say was "I will elope" - and that too in Hindi. All the five hundred people in the auditorium laughed at me. Then I heard someone say, "Please repeat the questions in Hindi for those people who don't understand English."

I was deeply embarrassed and that incident haunted me for many days. I tried to learn English, but I didn't have much success. What kept me going was that I did not want to do farming, work in the mills, or supply raw materials to factories. I wasn't exactly sure what I wanted to do, but I wanted to do something different, something that I would enjoy doing, though I wasn't sure exactly what that was back then. This thought motivated me to learn the language and I could soon speak a few words of English. Then, I found a job in a call centre, but was soon thrown out. The training team at that office said that my English was beyond repair. They said I was untrainable!

Thereafter, I worked for five companies, one after the other. Strangely, every one of the five either closed down or I was thrown out. Perhaps this was a signal that I was meant to do something different. It took me a while longer to decode that signal from the Universe. By then, I had repeatedly proved that I was a loser, not only to myself, but to everyone around me as well. I was jobless. My sense of failure was deeply ingrained in my mind. Every morning I would get ready and go out for interviews, knowing that I would not be able to crack even a single one. And as predicted, I would come home in the evenings, defeated. This probably sounds like a cheap plot straight out of an old Bollywood movie, but not when you are the protagonist and the cameras are missing! There seemed to be nothing left in the world, at least not for me. I did not ask for much. I did not dream big. I just wanted to live with a little dignity, and even that was denied.

Much later in life, when I looked back and analyzed those days, I realized that my area of reference were images from my childhood of my parents struggling, my friends struggling, my relatives struggling, of villagers working hard. These were what instilled the belief in me that life was hard and that there was not enough for everyone. There was a lack. I didn't even know that I had this belief until I met a few enlightened people and true masters who made me aware of what I was capable of doing. The biggest revelation was when I realized that I had everything, but first I would have to train myself on how to use my inner powers. The student in me was ready. One after the other, I started meeting the teachers who could train me and share their wisdom with me.

One of the most powerful teachers I met during my journey was Shree Nithya Shanti, a forest monk who now shares his teachings with people all around the world. When I first met him, I told him how inferior I felt when I met people who were more intelligent, more learned and better educated than me. I felt illiterate, and had no clue about how to fulfill my dreams.

When he heard this, Shree Nithya Shanti asked

me, "Can you ever compare a tabla to a sitar? A sitar to a guitar? A guitar to a flute?"

"No," I replied.

"Can a tomato be compared to a potato? A potato to a radish?"

I said no again.

He said, "Bhupendra, we are all human beings and there is no way we can be compared with each other. Each of us has a different role to play in this world. When we make comparisons, we insult our own creator indirectly, as we blame him for making us the way we are."

He further stated, "We are great the way we are. We have almost all the possible knowledge which we want, the only thing we need to learn is to connect to our own higher self."

I was confused, not understanding what Nithya Shanti was saying. I asked him what he meant. He said: "Can you answer this question of mine - how did Gautama Buddha, Bhagwan Mahaveer, and Swami Vivekananda get their immense knowledge? Do you think they read all the books in the Universe? Or did they have Google as their support system?"

I immediately said no.

He continued, "They acquired this knowledge by connecting to their inner self, by accessing their own powers of the brain, by learning to believe in their own judgments, and by having full faith in their creator."

From that day onwards, I started to follow the path my guru had shared with me. I started feeling great about myself and I started coming out of the belief which I had that there is a lack.

People with this kind of thought process don't achieve much from the Universe. They grow old and die merely attempting to live with some dignity.

2. Belief that there is enough of what they want.

When you aspire for more, you should simultaneously count your blessings - show some gratitude. It's good to want a brand-new car, but be thankful for the one you already have. If you aspire for a perfect body, be thankful for what you have. If you are deep in poverty, be thankful that you are still alive and accept that there must be a reason for it. Some people do face difficulties in life, but they recover by thinking positively. They make quick calculations of what they have and use those as a trampoline to bounce back.

A few people follow this belief, and guess what? They live happy and blissful lives.

Have you noticed that some people are less stressed than others, that they take life as it comes? These are the people who operate from this belief pattern, and I'm sure you will agree that this is a much better attitude to have than the previous one.

Here is another example from my experiences.

My sense of failure had demoralized me, and instead of preparing for my next job interview, I found myself planning an escape - suicide.

Yes, you read that right - I was planning to end my life. I explored various options of a painless death. I said to myself, "Is jumping from a tall building less painful than drowning? Shall I slit my wrist? Or should I just take sleeping pills?" I finally zeroed in on lying across a railway track and letting a locomotive do the rest. With that thought on my mind, I headed to the railway station when, by chance, I met a friend who persuaded me to accompany him to his friend's birthday party.

I joined him.

And that phase passed.

Later, I realized that killing myself would have done me no good. It would have just hurt my loved ones. I had no option but to take a U-turn or to bounce back. And that's exactly what I did - bounce back, bit by bit. Up until then, I had concentrated on what I did not have - I did not have a proper education, I did not have money, I couldn't speak English, I did not have a job. Then I thought, since I've made a list of what I *don't* have, why not make a list of what I do have? To begin with, I am alive and have a perfectly functional body and mind. Isn't that a good start? I have some education, some money and I'm young enough to make it all work.

Once I added that up, I realized that, for the first time in ages, I actually felt good about myself. And I made this a practice. I started to think that I had always got whatever I really wanted in my life. This thought relieved me from all my tensions and worries. I felt so peaceful. It made me feel that I was surrounded by blessings, that I was not alone. That my parents and friends loved me, and that I could always depend upon them. They were always there; it was only that I could not see them because I was busy counting my misfortunes. Slowly, I started counting my blessings, and this filled me with positive energy.

When I grew older and met my first guru, he shared with me one of the secrets to success in life. He said, "Keep a diary and write down ten achievements you have accomplished every day."

I replied, "Sir, until today I have never had ten achievements in my life and you are asking me to write ten every day!"

He replied, "Yes, ten every day. Those achievements can be very small, like bringing a smile to someone's face or giving someone a compliment."

What I like about myself and what I believe is the

main reason for my success is that I religiously follow whatever my trainer or guru says. And that's what I did.

I called my little diary my Victory Journal, and started listing ten small victories every single day, without fail.

Here are some extracts from my Victory Journal:

- Hurray! Today I reached the office on time.

- I have successfully finished my assignment and I am very happy about it.

- I felt great helping my friend repair his bike.

There was little effort but the effect was profound. It filled me with a feeling of goodness and well-being. I was happy.

By this time, I had the burning desire to learn English. All my ambitions to learn it had come to naught, but I knew I had to do it. I wanted to. So I started again, this time with a firm determination to succeed. Surprisingly, I started liking myself too. When I stood in front of the mirror, I saw a handsome man. It made me laugh happily!

I worked hard and had successfully taken the first step towards my destination.

I learned English, and I could speak it good enough to address a thousand people attending my sessions.

Good enough not to revert to Hindi when talking to people who spoke in English.

Good enough to forget that the language was not my mother tongue.

I was delighted. I now had more things to be thankful about at the end of the day and more points to add to my Victory Journal. I never realized that this small act could have had such a huge impact. It was changing me bit by bit and I could feel the change pulsing through me with renewed force every day.

It was during this time that I was introduced to a concept called the 'power of purpose.'

It is said that each person is born for a purpose. God did not send us to the Earth just to occupy space. And in order to fulfill that purpose, he has gifted everyone with something called *unique ability*.

Yes, with my experience I can tell you right now that you have one ability that is different from others. You can do at least one thing better than others; you have a special talent that differentiates you from others. The sooner you discover this, the better it will be for you. That's what all successful people do. They don't learn new things. They just harness that one unique ability they have, develop their strengths, and achieve success. Yes, that unique ability can't be created; it can only be discovered, as it is a part of you. Find it and then work on it. It's only through working on this unique ability that we can find happiness. And when we are happy in something, then we automatically excel in it.

So, stop, think, and ask yourself: what is your unique ability?

You don't know? Okay, then ask yourself what is it that your heart desires most? What is it that is consuming your thoughts and energy? Because whatever that is, it is probably your unique ability. Remember that whatever it is you desire may not be acceptable to the world at large. People will sometimes oppose you, make you look like a fool, discourage you, and coax you into giving it up. But this is your test. The Universe tests your desire before granting it to you. From time to time, it will also send you signals to check if you are right or wrong. You will need to decode these signals and march ahead. You need to trust the Law of Attraction and know that whatever it is you desire, the Universe will endeavor to give it to you.

Whenever I wanted to put the Law of Attraction into practice, I was confronted by many roadblocks. Nothing worked for me, or so I thought. I knew I could do it, but nothing happened. I had a job so that I could survive, but it wasn't something I wanted to do. I couldn't leave my job because how else would I make ends meet. My mind was filled with an endless barrage of questions, many of which were asked by others. I wanted to follow my heart, go with the flow, but those questions erected barriers around me.

I fought with myself and with the world around me. I was tired of fighting and was about to give up. Then one fine day, while I was riding my bike, I looked up at the sky and asked God what his plans were for me. I said, "Please, God, tell me if what I am doing is the right thing. Give me a signal. At least give me something that will tell me that I am on the right track."

Immediately, almost like an answer to my prayer, my cell phone rang. The caller asked if I was interested in conducting a three-day training program at WIPRO in Pune. That was it.

Eureka! I decoded this powerful signal from the Universe and acted upon it at once by conveying my decision to my family and resigning from my job. Yes, the Universe gives you signals at every point, but only those who are filled with a burning desire and want to learn, can decode those signals. I recommend that you master the art of learning how to decode the Universe's signals, because once you do so, your life will be a lot easier and you will start growing faster. Trusting the Universe is the only way to ensure that your life runs smoothly and that you rise with speed. This is the first important point I would like to make.

The second important thing is that the Universe loves speed. If you don't act the moment the thought hits you, then the thought will vanish and the momentum will break. So act immediately! When you have a thought and your heart convinces you that it is the right thought, then take action. When you decode a signal, don't waste time judging whether it's right or wrong, just follow whatever it is your heart tells you - go with the flow.

After that, I never looked back, never stopped, never gave up, never asked how or why. I have learned that these are meaningless questions that simply waste time. All we should do is have a burning desire and believe in it. That's all there is to it, and the Universe will provide.

Now, I would like you to do something I call the Power of 5. Believe me when I say that the Power of 5 has the capability to change your destiny.

This is what you need to do:

Keep a journal and write the following things in it every single day without fail:

5 big or small victories

I have already shared this with you, but you should remember to add at least one adjective like 'great' or 'wonderful' when you write these down. They will help you put your desires and thoughts into some kind of perspective, and if you continue this practice, you will notice that your thoughts and actions get more refined.

5 reasons why you should love yourself more today

All the great masters have had one remarkable ability - they could understand the power of self-love. If you can't love yourself, then why should the world love you? Here are some simple examples to help you appreciate yourself:

i)   I love myself because I helped a blind person cross the road.

ii) I love myself because I conserved a bucket of water.

iii) I love myself because I made someone happy today.

iv) I love myself because I wrote an article today.

5 of your desires

Put down the 5 desires you really want to be fulfilled. They can be big or small, wild or unrealistic - it really doesn't matter at all. Just write them down as if they have already been fulfilled and you are enjoying their benefits. Here are some examples:

i)   I have a wonderful limousine and my family and I enjoy travelling in it.

ii) I am a very famous personality.

iii) I am one of the richest men in the world.

iv) Everyone who meets me falls in love with me.

v) I can now fly high in the sky.

5 of the day's blessings

One of the most powerful ways of keeping your feet grounded and spirits high is to count your blessings. It instills in you a feeling of gratitude and as a result you feel rich and filled with abundance. And when you operate from this kind of attitude, abundance will be drawn towards you. A few examples:

i) I am thankful because my friend gave me a lift when my car broke down.

ii) I am thankful because a shopkeeper was courteous to me.

iii) I am thankful because my client admired my new shirt.

iv) I am thankful that I was able to afford a dinner in a five-star hotel.

Qualities that you would like to develop

Again, note down these qualities as if you already possess them. Some examples:

i) I am very honest and humble.

ii) I am a great leader.

iii) I take positive risks.

iv) I love others selflessly.

v)   I live up to my commitments.

vi) I am very energetic.

vii) I am very active.

Keep them to yourself and read them every day.

Learn to say "thank you." Say it often and say it with conviction. When you are thankful for certain things in your life, you are attracting more of those things back to you. You are concentrating on good things and they expand. So if you are grateful for the little money that you have, the small house you own, or the vintage car, you will be attracting more of everything to you - more money, a bigger house, a new car. This is the Law of Attraction at its simplest.

3. Belief that there is more than enough of what they want.

There are some people who just can't get enough. They are always excited and enthusiastic about everything around them. When they think, their thoughts flow freely without any barriers to restrict their dreams and desires. For them, the sky is the limit and everything in-between is theirs to claim. They are people with a no-limit personality and a no-limit mentality. They believe that the Universe has more than enough for everyone and that they just need to be there to receive it. They believe in receiving. For them it is unconceivable not to receive what they want. While some people like to choose and chase, they look at the Universe as an ocean of possibility. They throw their net of desire into this ocean with hope and faith and ask for everything their hearts desire.

These people are usually famous, remarkable people because they believed in the impossible.

In the past, these people included Albert Einstein, Thomas Alva Edison, Mahatma Gandhi, and Neil Armstrong. Today, people like Laxmi Mittal, Yuvraj Singh, Bill Gates, and Amitabh Bachchan continue to inspire us and to reaffirm that the Universe still creates people of this stature.

The Universe still says "I give you what you want" to everyone who follows the principle of the Law of Attraction.

Although there is more than enough in this world for everyone, the irony is that less than one percent of the people on Earth follow this belief. This is the reason why this tiny group of people holds 99 percent of the wealth and dominates the rest of the population. The truth is that the Universe and nature don't know what lack means. Only the human mind has created this concept of lack and abundance.

People who operate from this belief system live in a world of possibilities without a shred of fear. They don't doubt themselves or the Universe, because for them the thought "What if I don't get something?" has no meaning. They believe that the Universe will never say no, and if you know how to get tuned to its frequency, you will experience the harmony that only the Universe can provide.

Negative thoughts have negative effects on us, but not on others. This is because the thoughts are ours, the signals that we emit belong to us, and so they come back to us. If we wish for something bad to happen to another person, it won't touch that person. Instead it will come back to us because the thought was ours. But if we are trying to attract someone, that wish will be granted because by thinking of that person we are connecting with them.

Why is this so? Because we attract everything that comes into our lives by the virtue of the images we hold in our minds. We attract whatever is going on in our minds. Every thought of ours is a real thing - a force.

Once again, I would like to remind you of the virtue of positive thinking. I know you must have heard this a million times, but now you will understand its true meaning and its power.

All religions around the world talk about positive thinking. It has always been there for anyone to discover. It started at the beginning of time and will continue for eternity.

All places of worship have a unique aura of peace and serenity. Stress and tension swiftly disappear, the mind relaxes and the soul calms down. Even non-believers cannot deny their calming, almost therapeutic effect. Talk to the people who visit any place of worship regularly and they will tell you that they go there for 'peace of mind.' But how can a concrete structure like a temple or mosque or church or gurudwara give someone a greater sense of peace than their homes?

Here's how. The sense of unique peace and tranquility comes from all the positive thoughts and goodness that circulates through those places. No matter what a person's state of mind is, the moment they enter the house of God, all thoughts of revenge, hatred, anxiety, or tension vanish. They enter with a clean heart and pray for goodness. These positive thoughts collectively create positive vibrations that create an aura of happiness weaving little circles of happiness around the devotees. That's why even an abandoned structure hidden in a jungle can give a person a feeling of tranquility that even the grandest building can't.

Each moment of your life and every single thing you experience is determined by the Law of Attraction. It doesn't matter who you are or where you are. The law persists and it forms your entire life through your own thoughts! Right now! It is the greatest and the most infallible law upon which the entire system of creation depends.

There are some simple yet effective processes which can help you live in abundance and attract things faster.

- Appreciate yourself and the world around you.

- Live in gratitude.

- Feel good.

- Think big.

- Focus on what you want.

And they are as simple as they sound. Even implementing them is simple. But what stops us from implementing them is pure laziness. I am sure you are wondering why I am using such a defeatist word like 'laziness,' especially after laying down theories of success. Some of you must be frowning at the word and murmuring, "Hey, but I'm not lazy." But when you have in hand all the tools you need to be successful, and yet are not implementing them, what's stopping you? The various mind blocks and sheer laziness. Identifying your laziness and acknowledging it is equally important if you want to eradicate it from your system. This is explained further on in the book.

By the time you reach the end of this book, you will be able to successfully select and isolate all your strengths and weaknesses and use them to your advantage. So read on!

Have you ever wondered why rich people are rich? Or why it seems as though someone has everything and you have nothing? Or, worse still, have you ever wondered why God Almighty has given someone everything and you nothing? How unfair the one above is! Why is it that everything goes wrong with you, and only you?

Those who belong to the 'poor me' syndrome feel as if nothing is in their power, that fate or destiny have conspired to bog them down.

"My mother is terminally ill. My wife is going to have yet another baby. I wasn't given the promotion that was due to me. My car has suddenly developed engine problems. That influential person who was supposed to help me is out of town. The weather is terrible. The food is rotten. I have a headache and backache. I can't sleep, either..."

Have you ever grumbled like that, or come across people during an office break who open up a Pandora's Box of woes? You must have listened to their stories sympathetically, offered words of comfort, maybe extended a helping hand. Well, next time, don't!

Don't get me wrong. I'm not asking you to be rude. But be a true friend by telling them that all their troubles have been brought about by their own thoughts. Offer to help by asking them to choose their thoughts from now on and to be positive about everything for the next thirty days, no matter what happens. And then watch the magic! And I do call it magic. It doesn't matter if you can't see the magician's wand or the hopeful colors of your thoughts sending signals to the Universe. It's definitely there with all its benevolent force.

2

Reticular Activating System (RAS)

There is a portion of the brain called the reticular activating system (RAS) that allows you to choose and make decisions. The RAS plays an important role in a person's ability to achieve his goals.

To understand what the RAS is, let me give you an example.

Imagine you are at a very crowded fair with your spouse. It's like a madhouse - noisy and confused with music blaring everywhere and people shouting at the top of their voices. In the middle of it all, you suddenly lose contact with your partner. You are frantically searching for them. There is a lot of noise around but you ignore the sounds as you search. Suddenly you hear your name being announced over the microphone amidst the booming noise, and your attention is caught. How could this happen?

There is an automatic mechanism in your brain - the RAS - that brings relevant information to your attention immediately. It is like a filter between your conscious and subconscious mind. It takes instructions from your conscious mind and passes them on to the subconscious mind.

Say you fall asleep in a room full of people with the TV operating in full volume and the sound of traffic audible through the window. Nothing disturbs you until someone calls your name. You respond to it immediately without being consciously aware of it.

That's because the RAS responds to certain preset instructions and most people are alerted when their names are mentioned. So while the subconscious filters out all the other noises, it chooses to pick out your name and act on it.

So why do I say 'choose'? That's because we can deliberately program the RAS to choose the exact message from the conscious mind - like setting a goal or affirming or visualizing the goal.

It is said that we can achieve any realistic goal by thinking about it long enough and stop thinking anything negative about it.

This means that if our thoughts say that we will not achieve our goal, our reticular activating system will see to it that we do not achieve it because the dominant thought here is 'not.'

So what we need to do is create a very definite picture of our goals in our conscious mind. The picture then passes over to the subconscious, which automatically attracts or brings to our attention all relevant information that we would have been oblivious of otherwise. It also filters out what is unnecessary.

So if you want to create your own destiny, get your RAS to work, because it is the RAS that decides on what you are focusing your attention.

The Law of Attraction says like attracts like. So you will attract what you think in your life. So if you are thinking about money, you will attract more money, sometimes in mysterious ways. You may receive a cheque from a fixed deposit that has just matured, or a letter from a forgotten aunt who has bequeathed all her wealth to you! If you are worried about losing money, you will find that all your money is being siphoned away by something or the other, whether you like it or not. If you are thinking of illness, you will never be perfectly fit and healthy. If nothing else, you will always be plagued by a persistent headache. If you are thinking of love, you will receive love. But if your thoughts say, "I love that person so much, but that person doesn't love me at all," no matter how hard you try, you will never get your desired love. If you fear that the three topics that you did not revise for your examination will appear in the question paper, guess what? They will definitely be there. If you fear that your car will break down in the middle of nowhere, then it will surely happen. Whatever your predominant thoughts are, they will materialize.

Remember the story of Aladdin and his magic lamp, in which a genie pops out whenever the magic lamp is rubbed and says, "Your wish is my command!" Like in the Aladdin story, the magic lamp is your mind and the genies are your innumerable wishes. You activate those wishes every time you think about them. That's what the power of your mind is. Every time you make a wish, the genie says, "Your wish is my command!" This demonstrates how you have created your entire life. The genie will answer your every command, assuming that that's what you want. It could be positive or negative, good or bad; whatever it is that is dominating your thoughts. If you can see it in your mind, you will be holding it in your hands soon.

If you dream about driving a red car even though you are forced to travel in overcrowded buses all the time, you are going to get one sooner or later. The only condition is that you need to make a commitment to yourself about having it, and to believe in that commitment. This is visualization. This is an essential step that fast-tracks you towards the realization of your dreams.

Believe that you have the car. Touch it. Feel it. Imagine that you are inserting the key to open the door to the driver's seat. Grip the black-leather steering wheel. Hear the car start up as you turn on the ignition. See it roll out of the parking lot and zoom onto the streets. Do this every day and it won't be long before that car stands in front of your doorstep. Don't belive me? Try it! It's the Law of Attraction. It never fails!

Thoughts are magnetic in nature and have a frequency that attracts all thoughts of the same frequency. Everything sent out returns to the source, and the source is you!

When we surf through the various channels on television, what do we exactly do? We change the frequency. Every channel is broadcasted from the television station's transmission tower via a frequency, and in order to view it, we need to match that frequency with the television set in our house. When we want to see something different, we change the channel and tune into a new frequency.

We are a human transmission tower, and we are more powerful than any television tower created by any human being. Since we are a creation of the Universe, the frequency we transmit goes beyond cities, beyond countries, and the world. It reverberates throughout the entire Universe. And we are transmitting that frequency with our thoughts!

So the pictures you receive from the transmission of your thoughts are the pictures of your life! Your thoughts create the frequency, attract things at the same frequency, and broadcast them back to you as your life's picture. If you want to change anything in your life, first change your thoughts.

"The world we have created is the product of our thoughts. It cannot be changed without changing our thinking." - Albert Einstein

But this 'changing of thoughts' is easier said than done. If you consciously monitor your thoughts for a single day, you will realize that there is a definite pattern to it. Research says that people think about sixty thousand thoughts per day! These thoughts have a definite pattern, depending on various factors. These factors can be broadly divided into two categories: positive thoughts and negative thoughts.

There are some people who always engage in negative thoughts. Even if something good happens to them, they disregard it by thinking that it's time for something bad to take place. They 'forget' how to be happy. They send negative signals to the Universe, and keep sending them until something truly dreadful happens, and then they wisely claim, "See, I knew it was coming! For every single laugh, they are forced to cry ten times over."

They wake up in the morning and say, "Oh, I'm late again." They then go to the bathroom and crib about the damp towel, the wet floor, the lukewarm tea, the meagre breakfast, the heavy traffic, the bad weather - everything is negative for them. They crib and complain throughout the day until they go to bed at night. When they try to be positive, they just end up justifying themselves. You will notice that such people never see the light of happiness till the end of their lives. Theirs is always a sob story. When you ask them, "Hey! How are you?" their response will never be the usual, "I'm fine, how are you?" They will instead hand you a detailed medical report with their complicated medical history.

On the other hand, there are people whom I call bouncers. They seem to carry a trampoline around with them. No matter what the situation is, they somehow always manage to bounce back. Even when something bad happens, they treat it as a 'temporary situation' and know for sure that it's going to change for better.

We assume that these people are always happy as they never complain about anything. We don't realize that this is because they don't let bad things hover around them for too long, like a humming bird hovering around a flower. Any bad occurrence is overpowered by the power of their positive thoughts. They push through mishaps with their immense positive energy. They believe in their abilities and have complete faith in the Universe. And once their strong signals are sent to the Universe, it conspires to say 'amen.'

Here is a story my mother told me long ago, which has since had a huge impact on my life.

This was when my mother was studying in college. Behind her parental home was a rocky hill where domestic staff like maids, cooks, and others lived in their little huts. One day, during monsoon, there was a terrible landslide and huge boulders tumbled down from the top of the hill crushing the huts below. A few people died in the tragedy. Amongst the people affected by the disaster were two families, who were neighbors. Both had a similar family structure - a husband, a wife, and a son and a daughter, both of the same age group. Their kids went to the same school in their locality. Each family owned a shop at the end of the lane on the foothills. They sold miscellaneous items like groceries, stationery, some medicines, and the like. The turnover was such that they could barely sustain themselves.

Both their houses were completely destroyed in the mishap - not even a pot or pan could be saved. My mother says that although one family wailed and cried incessantly, the other sulked for a while but soon bounced back by counting their blessings. "My family is safe," the father would say. "Nothing happened to my shop. I am grateful to God for his mercy."

While the other man fretted over his massive loss, his neighbor started rebuilding his home and business from the scraps that were left. His wife took up sewing and cleaning while he ran the shop. He did not allow his kids to miss school even for a single day, and as a result they could appear for their final examinations that were just round the corner.

His neighbor, on the other hand, did not manage to reopen his shop for several months, and appealed to his well-to-do neighbors for monetary help. In the beginning, people sympathized and lent a helping hand, but soon lost interest. Their kids dropped out of school. The other two kids did well in their studies, and when the community saw how hard they were trying, they would also try to help them from time to time. The local boys' club took the responsibility of supplying them with textbooks, uniforms, and stationary, while the school exempted them from paying the school fees. Clothes and utensils were donated whenever the need arose. They were always thankful for whatever they received, unlike the other family who were never happy with what they got and would constantly want something more or something else.

Years later, when I last went home, my mother informed me that the family who had never stopped believing and living in gratitude and faith had received their dues from the Universe. Their daughter was to be married to a pilot, a friend of her brother's. The daughter was teaching at one of the A-grade English schools in the city. My mother said that when the father came over to invite us for the wedding, she asked if he was happy now that his children were doing well in life. His reply took her by surprise. He said, "I have never been unhappy. In fact, I made sure that I was always happy with my lot in my life. That's what has sustained me and my family for so long."

"What happened to his friend and his children?" I asked my mother, curious of their fate.

My mother replied, "Their father has lung cancer and is now bedridden. Their mother too is ailing, probably as a result of malnutrition. The son tries to run the small shop they had, but now that there are better and bigger shops just round the corner, nobody visits his shop. The daughter takes care of the household chores. The children are working hard to support the family. We all tried to help in the beginning, but the father refused to pull himself together. Slowly we all gave up."

She added casually, "One shouldn't blame them totally for their misfortune. Somehow it seemed as if destiny had abandoned them. Even though things went off well with their neighbor, it looked as if God never gave them a thought. The father, who was the only earning member of the family, fell prey to a terrible disease. Their mother couldn't go out to work because she hadn't been keeping well since the mishap. One bad thing led to another and they could never recover from the mishap."

Does this story ring a bell? For me it does when I apply the Law of Attraction to interpret the situation. While one of them kept his faith and his thoughts aligned with the Universe, the other magnified his misfortune, concentrated on his loss, and tuned his thoughts to all the negative vibrations of the Universe.

The Law of Attraction said *tathastu* to both of them!

You need to monitor your thoughts and recognize their patterns. If you are someone who tends to be happier rather than sad throughout the day, then you are in line with the positive energy of the Universe. If you are grateful for all things big and small, if you know how to keep your faith and never lose hope, then no matter what your present troubles are, good times are just around the corner.

Having said that, it is really difficult to monitor all sixty thousand thoughts one by one and analyze them. So what can you do? Well, there is a trick. Stop - now! And ask yourself, how are you feeling? Are you happy at this moment, or are you sad? Because you cannot be happy and have negative thoughts simultaneously, or, for that matter, feel angry and think positive. It's simply not possible.

Please understand this, for this is true - there is no way you can attract good in your life with negative thoughts or do bad to yourself with lots of positive thoughts. Put aside this book for a couple of minutes and think. Think about all the bad things that have happened in your life, and also the good ones. Whenever you had a 'hunch' or an 'insight' that something would happen ("I knew it!"), dear reader, you were asking for it. Even begging for it persistently until you yourself made it happen.

You need to make this a practice. Stop every now and then, abruptly, and do a mood check. This will tell you about your flow of thoughts. If you find yourself depressed or frustrated, then your signals are negative. If you are upbeat, happy, and energetic, then your signals are positive. Be sure that something good is going to happen. Maybe that pretty girl or that handsome guy you spotted in the office canteen yesterday will walk up to you and say "Hi!" Just a thought, really!

3

How to Convert Your Negative Beliefs into Positive Ones

If you continue to have negative thoughts for a long time, then there is a risk that you may create a negative belief. Some people are blessed with the attributes that can help them grow, but many times they are not able to do so because of the negative, limiting beliefs they have harbored. These beliefs are so harmful that they can kill all your creative instincts and block all the ways that can lead you to freedom and abundance. These beliefs just weaken you and rob you of your powers.

If you find that your mood is consistently negative, change it. Break these negative beliefs as soon as possible. But before you jump into the breaking of negative beliefs, let's start with what these beliefs are and how they are formed. Here is a beautiful story of how beliefs can be formed and how they can affect us.

Once upon a time, there lived a wise old monk. Other monks who learned divine practices from him lived there as well. This wise old monk had a pet cat that he loved. Every time, the monk and his disciples would sit and meditate, the monk would tie his cat near him to stop him from running around and disturbing the others. This carried on for almost thirty years until the old monk passed away.

He was succeeded by a senior monk, and for some reason they continued to tie the cat before they started meditation. One day they couldn't find the cat and this disturbed them because their meditation seemed incomplete without the animal. As a result, finding the cat became more important than the meditation itself.

All the monks believed that the wise old man used to tie the cat because there was some logic or reason behind it; that it was an essential part of group meditation. Not having the cat was perceived as a breach of rituals. It felt ominous! Their mediation could not be successful without the cat.

What is the inference from the story? Someone did something for his own convenience and the other people blindly believed that there was a purpose to it.

That's how beliefs are formed.

If you hold a thought and you have enough experience to validate that thought, then that thought becomes a belief. For example, if you think you are wise and people come to you and appreciate you for your wisdom, then with time you develop the belief that you are indeed very wise. And the longer this goes on, the stronger this belief becomes. Beliefs get developed very easily and they get ingrained in your system before you even realize it.

Such beliefs fall under two categories - the ones that motivate us and the ones that pull us down. The former are called empowering or positive beliefs and the latter are called limiting or negative beliefs.

It is good to nurture the positive beliefs, but is it also important to eradicate the limiting or negative beliefs.

Below is a six-step process on how you can get rid of your negative beliefs.

1. *Identify the negative belief.*

2. *Stop reinforcing it with immediate effect.*

3. *Understand that beliefs are not facts.*

4. *Doubt and challenge the negative belief.*

5. *Think about the empowering belief with which you would like to replace this negative belief.*

6. *Condition your mind with the empowering belief.*

Let's start with the first step.

1. Identify the negative belief.

First you need to learn how to identify your negative beliefs.

To do so you need to first recognize the negative thoughts that are strong in your mind and then validate them by asking few questions. For example, you think, "I am not good at studies."

- Is this a recurring thought?
- Does it make you feel bad?
- Is it stopping you from taking some action towards reaching your goal?
- How else does it stop your growth?

Negative thoughts are those that create a negative impact in your life. So recurring thoughts that make you feel bad or restrict you can be a negative belief.

2. Stop reinforcing it with immediate effect.

Without really being aware, people keep reinforcing their negative beliefs by collecting false evidence that support them, and by thinking about them over and over.

Both actions reinforce the negative belief and make it stronger. The first step to change a negative belief is to stop reinforcing it. You need to start by changing your perception of events and by not thinking about them over and over again.

3. Understand the difference between facts and beliefs.

Understand that beliefs are not facts. There is a huge difference between a fact and a belief. Facts never change, but beliefs do. Facts are the same for everyone, but beliefs depend on the person. For example, it is a fact that Shah Rukh Khan is a huge celebrity, but it is a belief that no one can be greater than him.

So don't think that your beliefs are the only way of living. Your beliefs are just one paradigm. Shift your paradigm and you will see just how beautiful the world is.

4. Doubt and challenge the negative belief.

One of the best ways to change a negative belief is to challenge it and doubt it.

Some people who come to my workshops tell me that they are not confident. I ask them what makes them believe that they are not confident, and they provide me with a list of incidents to prove their statement. I ask them the following questions to challenge their own negative beliefs:

- How do you know that you are not confident?

- Are you sure that you are not confident?

- Have you never been confident in your life?

- Don't you remember even a single situation in your life when you were confident?

- Can you doubt this belief of yours?

- Would you still lack confidence if your life or your family members' life is dependent on you doing the right thing?

Once, when I was addressing a group of over a thousand students, I noticed that a large clump of students were sitting together and not participating. This was lowering the overall energy levels of the room, so I had to do something about it. I invited a few of them to come on the stage to volunteer for an activity, but there was no response. I kept persuading but it did not work.

Then, I got down from the stage and walked through the audience and again requested for a few to volunteer for the activities. They refused. I got a chair and sat down in front of one student. My microphone was on so everyone could listen to what we were talking about. I asked him, "Why don't you want to come on the stage?"

He replied, "I have never been on the stage and that's why I am scared."

"So how will the fear go away? Can it go away by just sitting in the corner in a chair?"

"No.."

"Well, do you want to be successful or you want to remain ordinary?"

"I want to be very successful."

"Will you ever be successful by being fearful?"

"No."

"How long do you think you want to live the same life which is full of fear?"

The reply came quickly. "Not even a single minute more."

"So why don't you come and face this fear from the stage?"

"No, I won't come. I'm afraid."

Hearing this, I gave him the following hypothetical situation: "If you reach home this evening and find your mom on her deathbed and her last wish is to see you on stage, speaking in front of a huge audience, and receiving a standing ovation, would you not fulfill that wish?"

"Of course I would!"

This gave me the chance to ask my next set of questions. "How do you know that your mom is going to live forever? Do you know how many people are losing their parents right at this moment?"

I got up and walked back up to the stage after asking these questions - and the student followed me up. And so did all those other people who refused to volunteer.

Challenging your negative beliefs reduces its power over you. Can you challenge your negative beliefs? Can you ask yourself some powerful questions to shake your own thoughts and bring out the best in yourself?

5. Think about the empowering belief that will replace this negative belief.

Can you now start saying, "I am the most confident guy in the world"? Can you start saying this with a lot of confidence and emotion? If yes, then you will be able to turn the negative belief into a positive one. Similarly, turn all your negative beliefs into positive ones, one by one. Follow step six if you have done this.

6. Condition your mind with the empowering belief.

Now is the time to program your mind with the new empowering belief. This can be done as follows:

- Repeat the empowering belief as many times as possible. This is called affirmation. Catch yourself during all those times when you are living this positive belief. This will create a referral point in your mind. Create many such referral points to strengthen the belief.

- People who are role models are those who already follow this empowering belief. Try to imitate them and live like they do. Try to map their thoughts and beliefs. Match their actions and words. This will speed up the entire process.

- Change something in the outer world as soon as possible. This means start doing things that remind you about the positive beliefs.

It is practically criminal to have negative beliefs. If you have many negative beliefs then you are murdering your true self. You are putting yourself in an invisible cage that will never allow you to remain free. You are undervaluing yourself and limiting your own powers.

Well, what are you waiting for? Discover each and every negative belief and shatter them right at this moment. Yes, I mean it. Right here, right now! Close this book and take over your negative beliefs one by one.

4

The Formula for Successful Manifestation

Have you noticed that people who are in love rarely have a sad story to tell? Everything seems to be in sync around them. When they talk to their friends, they will never grumble about anything. New lovers are almost never ill and all of a sudden they find themselves attracting many new things in their life, such as new friends, a new job, a congenial workplace, a booming business and so on. We say Lady Luck smiled on them.

But do you know the real secret? Of all the feelings and emotions known to mankind, love is the strongest. When you are in love, you emit such strong vibrations that everything gets attracted to you with the speed of light. Now we can comprehend the reason behind the age-old saying, "Love makes the world go round." Well, you never thought it was so literal, right?

When I say love, I don't mean the romantic kind. I mean love for everything. It could be for that little red car which you desperately wanted, or that dream project you've had since you were a kid, or your wish to visit Scotland. You loved it with all your being and then it manifested in your life. This is nothing but the Law of Attraction yet again!

You might say, "That's true. But how does this actually work? Can you actually make things happen? I work so hard and I am ready to do whatever it takes, but nothing seems to get me my heart's desire."

That's because there is a process to be followed, some knowledge to be gained, and skills to be practiced. Nnow let's increase our awareness towards a few things and find out how and why the law of attraction works. Once we know this, we can easily apply it in our daily lives.

Each one of us has the desire to be successful and achieve great heights in our lives. But many times we get lost in the rut and lack direction in life to reach our goal.

Below are four points that will give you a sense of direction and have a profound effect on your life.

1. *Burning desire*

2. *Absolute clarity*

3. Conviction

4. Hope and faith

Let's start with the first one.

1. Burning desire

The law of attraction says that if you have a burning desire, there's nothing in this world that you cannot achieve. The only condition is that this desire has to be strong and needs to be conveyed to the Universe in the most positive way.

Affirmation is the first and the most important step towards realizing your burning desire.

To start with, you need to have to wish for something you want very dearly. The Universe is waiting for you to ask your wish.

All you need to do is express your wildest dream; and affirm it with all the strength of your thoughts. Focus on that thought and only that thought alone. Don't try to analyze your wish. Don't try to be considerate and dilute it. Don't minimize it or settle for something lesser. It will be foolish to do so when the Universe is there to grant it to you.

Think about this scenario. The baby Neil Armstrong took small, stumbling steps towards his mother, sucking his thumb and says that he wants to walk on the moon. His mother must have picked him up, kissed him, and laughed at his wish. But as an adult, when he still wished to travel to the moon, his mother must have swooned at his son's unusual ambition. But today, we all know who that man is. Did you think his dream was a little eerie? Well, not anymore. So just do this much for yourself - be fearless and ask for whatever desire is burning in your heart.

But remember that this Universe is very intelligent. It doesn't just believe in what you think your burning desire is. The moment you claim that you have a burning desire, the Universe will put you through a series of tests. The one who clears all these tests is the one who conquers it all.

Here I want to grab an opportunity to share one of my experiences with you. When I attended many self-help programs, I got to see a 360-degree change in my life. I got to see that all my weaknesses were turning into my strengths, one by one. My teachers inspired me and I developed the desire to become a breakthrough expert, a coach, and a life transformer. Every time I attended the sessions, this feeling grew stronger. I immediately wanted to take a different route. All of a sudden my IT job stopped exciting me, and my thoughts were focused towards transforming human lives. I was burning with this particular desire to become a catalyst for change.

Then came the testing time. The Universe started putting me through a series of tests that I passed with flying colors, and today I am living a life of bliss.

The major test I went through was to convince my parents and my friends, to leave my job to follow my heart completely. There were many practical challenges: my job was really good, and I was earning a handsome salary. So justifying quitting my job was a challenge. And if I quit, there would be no financial support from anywhere else. I didn't know how would I survive without a steady source of income. How long it would take for me to start earning money in my new field of interest? I wasn't even sure who would attend my program since I was new to the profession. There were many big names at that time and very few people knew me in the city.

It was a scary test as my entire life depended upon it but I was determined. I started thinking about the worst-case scenarios. I realized that the worst which could happen was that I might lose a few lakhs and I might need to return to my IT job after a couple of years. "If that's it," I thought, "I might as well give it a shot."

Luckily, I had a lakh in cash stashed away and I thought it should be enough for me to survive for a year. After brainstorming for a while, I finally took a leap of faith. I listened to my heart and jumped into this unknown field.

My parents didn't understand why I wanted to change my profession and venture into unknown territory. I faced strong resistance, but when the desire is fuelled by passion you always believe in yourself and follow it through. I took my decision and moved ahead. Yes, my family members were initially hurt by my apparent indifference to their opinions, and they conveyed their view to me. But I was glad that I could clear this test.

There were times when my belief about my own abilities was shaken. I would be scared. At those times, there was one quote that gave me hope. It made me strong and helped me take action even when I was scared. And that was this:

"It's not that winners are not scared. Winners win because they take actions in spite of the fear."

This decision of mine was an affirmation to the Universe that yes, I had a burning desire - the desire to make a huge difference to the world around me.

It has been said that if you really want something with all your heart then the entire Universe will conspire to give it to you. That's what started happening ever since I took this big, bold, and brilliant step. Yes, I call it a brilliant step because if I had been my previous self, I would never have been able to take this step and would have continued in a job I did not like, with no freedom to operate from my own heart.

If you search deep within, you will realize that it is fear and fear alone that stops us from dreaming and turning those dreams into burning desires. For example, a person who earns just fifty thousand per year would be petrified of dreaming about owning a Jaguar. He will not even allow himself to dream about it, thinking, "What's the point? I will only make myself miserable. I will never be able to own such a car. Not even with my entire life's earnings." Forget about wanting to acquire it, he will be terrified even to dream about it or admire it!

Ask yourself this question - what is that one thing you would have wanted to do if fear did not exist?

Fear is a big hurdle, deep-rooted in the conscious and the subconscious mind, perhaps because of some past experience or acquired knowledge. Most of us are terrified of cockroaches even though they don't bite and are not poisonous. This is fear. This fear will hold you back. Of all the fears known to mankind, fear of failure is the top one. No matter what you set out to achieve, fear of failure comes first to your mind, even before the joy of a possible success, and makes the journey an uphill task, for you are constantly fighting the unseen. While the fear of failure is natural, it is important to remember that we should not let the fear of a possible failure overpower the joy of a possible success. It's foolish, time-consuming, and absolutely useless. To make your mind focus on positive affirmations is vital. The more you affirm to the Universe with full faith and conviction, the more you systematically obliterate the fear of failure. Just as two contradictory emotions on the same subject cannot stay together or hold the same strength. One has to die to let the other live. Methodical affirmation makes sure that your dream survives and the thought of not achieving it fades away.

2. Absolute clarity

This is my favorite topic for when I ask people what their goal in life is. Most people say that they want more money. So I immediately take out a thousand-rupee note from my pocket, show it to them, and say, "Look, now your goal is accomplished! You have more money than you did a minute ago."

Laughing, the person replies, "No, when I say I want more, I mean a lot more." I ask him to define how much "a lot more" is. There's no answer because no one is certain about how much more they want. Similarly, many people say that their goal is to be peaceful, or to be happy in life.

And I ask them, how do you measure happiness and peace? How would the Universe know that you are perfectly happy now, or feeling at peace? And why should it single you out when everyone is asking for the same thing?

Clarity is key. If there is no clarity, then there is no manifestation.

There should be no ambiguity and no waffling. You should be absolutely clear about what you want. Like at this moment, I want to finish writing this book and get it published. The link between feelings, actions, words, emotions, and thoughts should not be broken. One broken link will mean that you have doubts and this will weaken the signals. You will be sending mixed-color signals to the Universe. There will be streaks of black mixed with the bold red of positive intent, and it is the amount of black that will determine anything between delay and denial. This signal of mixed colors will confuse the Law of Attraction, and it will not have the desired degree of manifestation.

The Law of Attraction works every time. It never fails. Like the law of gravity, the Law of Attraction is universal and always in force.

Try out this simple experiment. Get a bar magnet and some iron filings. A magnet has two poles: positive and negative. One end is marked P, for positive, and the other is N, for negative. Now scatter a few iron filings on a sheet of paper and place the magnet directly under the paper.

You will notice how all the filings gather together just above the magnet. Keep moving the magnet and watch how the filings scatter and gather again. We know that the positive end is attracted to the negative and vice versa. Now if you take the positive end of the magnet and slowly run it under the paper in one direction, you will observe that the iron filings arrange themselves beautifully and strictly in order with all the positive poles at one end and the negative poles at the other.

Now try flipping the magnet and switching the poles. What happens? The iron filings dance merrily on the piece of paper, forgetting the rules that binds them. You have confused them.

This is exactly what will happen if you keep sending mixed signals to the Universe. You make them dance without direction, and at the end, there will be minimum results, or no results, or even negative results. That's when you say, "See, I knew it wouldn't work. I always knew it wouldn't." But what you don't realize is that your doubt has manifested itself.

Obeying the Law of Attraction will give you what you ask for.

3. Conviction

We need a lot of conviction, or in other words, we need to believe in ourselves. What you think about, you bring about.

A shortcut to the manifestation of your desire is that you must see what you want for it to become an absolute fact. For this, people apply two categories of thought:

- Have-Do-Be
- Be-Do-Have

The Have-Do-Be people are the ones we call the ordinary people.

These people need to *have* everything in order to *do* something before they can become what they want to *be*.

For example, Have-Do-Be people who aspire for a muscular physique like that of Salman Khan would first run to the sports shop and buy all the necessary equipment. Then they would enroll in a gym. Then they would have to take time out from their work and daily routine to visit the gym every morning. And they would need a special diet and a good night's sleep.

Anything missing would be perceived as a huge hurdle and would thus prevent them from achieving their goal. These could be that they did not get the desired sportswear and shoes, or that the gym was too far from their house or was too badly equipped. Perhaps their work or the weather kept them away from their daily workout, or they couldn't follow their diet without supervision. All these will become insurmountable obstacles in the way of their success and they will fail every time. And they will successfully find someone else or something else to blame. What they fail to understand was that no one can control or dictate external factors. Others are not responsible for your success. What is responsible for their success or failure lies within them.

The other category is the Be-Do-Have people. They too were once ordinary people who made themselves extraordinary by turning the tables on themselves. If such people want to become like Salman Khan they think of themselves as Salman Khan from day one. They visualize their physiques like Salman Khan's. They also visualize the benefits of that amazing physique. They hear those compliments well in advance and can feel the benefits in the present. As a result, the doing part becomes automatic for them. They don't have to push themselves for any physical activity. They go to the gym if possible; if not, they run in their backyards, they run along railway tracks, they lift boulders and sandbags to build their muscles, and join chairs to do push-ups. They hang onto anything they can to do their pull-ups. They make themselves conscious about their diet, but they don't become too obsessed with it and stay focussed of their goal. Finally, they become what they want to be - a Salman Khan.

These categories of people do not wait for opportunities to knock on their doors. These people turn the wheel and make things happen. Everything else falls in place.

Let me ask you this: have you ever followed the Be-Do-Have pattern? I'm pretty sure you have. In fact, you followed it every single day when you were a kid. You wanted to play and you really wanted to become the best on that playing field. Did you ever think, "Oh! Playing means too much running and wasting energy, and it will take too much of time."

Unknowingly you wanted to have lots of fun. You played hard, you were exhausted, but you still wanted to keep playing. Ultimately you got what you wanted and that was a lot of happiness, satisfaction, and peace. In short, as a child, you lived every single day according to the Be-Do-Have way. This is the real secret of success which every great sportsman, businessman, bodybuilder, and filmmaker follows. In fact, all those people who are in the top one percent bracket live according to this philosophy.

Have-Do-Be and Be-Do-Have are very powerful concepts. You need to recognize your pattern - and no cheating, please! Then turn it around to your advantage. It's really very easy once you have correctly analyzed and acknowledged your category and helped yourself.

This thought process of pretending you've already become what you want to be is a good way to press down the conviction pedal at full throttle. So once you start believing that what you want is absolute, you need to behave accordingly. If it's a red car that you have asked the Universe for or a much-coveted academic achievement, you should have absolute conviction and make room to receive it - perhaps a garage in your backyard or a hallowed place in your personal wall of fame to hang mementos of your achievements. If it's that much-awaited job for which you were interviewed, buy new clothes and shoes to wear to the office. Or if you want to get married, make room in your life to accommodate that person when they come into your life. Once you have conviction in your wish, then the whole Universe will conspire to give it to you. Don't ask why or how. That's not your problem. Your job is to ask for it, have total clarity and conviction in it, and make room to receive it.

The strength of your signals with which you follow the above three steps determines how soon, how effectively and how generously your wish will be fulfilled.

No Doubt = Quick Manifestation

Some Doubt = Slow Manifestation

Lots of Doubt = No Manifestation

A very dear friend of mine used to say, "You know what? Someday I will receive a presidential award. In our sitting room, there will be a huge laminated photograph of me receiving an award from the President of India."

I laughed. We were then in the sixth standard and my friend was an extremely poor student. He would barely scrape through to the next standard. His report card always showed up in red.

"For consistently having red circles in your report card?" I used to tease him.

He was a dear friend and never took my teasing to heart. But what I didn't know was that behind his statement was a powerhouse of conviction. With each passing year, his grades improved considerably. Later, when he was doing his masters in botany, I visited him at his house and saw a large empty photo frame standing on his study table. I asked him what it was for. He smiled and said it was for that photograph of him with the president. "And I am so excited that it is APJ Abdul Kalam. He is the best president India has ever had!"

I thought my friend had lost his mind, and the confidence with which he said it made it even scarier.

Then during his M. Sc. finals, I went to his house again and saw the same photo frame hanging on his sitting room wall, still empty. This time I was really worried about him. You don't predict achievements of such magnitude. I mean who wouldn't want to receive an award from the president of his country for his achievements? But his strength of conviction had a crazy edge to it - or so I thought. But I was wrong! Today, that photo frame is adorned with a photograph of our glorious president shaking hands with my very dear friend while receiving the gold medal for his excellent performance in his academic field and his overall contribution to the field of science!

He made a wish, affirmed it to the Universe over and again, had total clarity about it, had conviction in it and received it by making room for it in his life. He had felt it in his hand even before he had actually received it and his dream materialized. This is a very simple example of the power of the mind and the power of the universal energy.

4. Hope and faith

President Obama of the United States won the election and became the president based on those two words. He gave hope to the people and showed them that they need to have faith in their own abilities. Not only had he given hope and faith to others, he was himself very hopeful and that's how the book called *The Audacity of Hope* came into existence. His subconscious had zero doubt in the ability of the Universe to deliver what he wanted.

These two words are very important. At no point in time can we lose hope and faith. I know that these words have been used so often that they have lost their strength. But try achieving something without either of them and see what happens.

Hope and faith are the two strong pillars that sustain you in the gestation period of making a wish and achieving it.

Hope and faith are what keep you going. They are what help you reach your goal. If you are building your dream house, trying unsuccessfully to invent something, or baking your first chocolate cake, you need to keep hope alive and have faith. These terms of serenity will allow you to realize your dream and let you follow your heart, step by step, till you achieve your goal.

I would like to add that if you have followed the first three steps, then you would automatically be able to have a great amount of hope and faith.

We have seen people conquer heaven, hell, and the earth in between with this very strength that we have just discussed: a burning desire that is strongly supported by absolute clarity, conviction, hope, and faith.

Every time this system has been followed, knowingly or unknowingly, the Universe has stood up in reverence and said: "So be it!"

Man wanted to eat tasty food, and so he discovered fire! He wanted to travel faster, so he invented the wheel! The Wright Brothers wanted to soar like a bird, so they invented the aeroplane! Alexander Graham Bell wanted to speak to people around the globe, so he invented the telephone! Neil Armstrong landed on the Moon! Tenzing Norgay was the first person to climb Mount Everest! Sher Shah Suri fought and killed a tiger with his bare hands! A mother tore open a wolf's mouth when she spotted her child in its killing jaws!

These are all examples of the immense power of the mind and human body. Sometimes we consciously make an effort to exercise it, and sometimes when we find ourselves thrown into adverse situations, we wonder how in the world we did it!

Two years ago, I read this item in the newspaper. Now listen closely, for every word is true.

A heavily pregnant woman was travelling in the train. Late at night she visited the washroom. While she was using it, her baby slipped from the womb and fell onto the track below. The train was speeding along, but the woman ran to the door, opened it, and jumped out. The train sped by as she ran back half a kilometer and picked up her baby from the track. The iron rails, the newspaper reported, were still burning hot. By that time the passengers had stopped the train and they rushed to the spot where the woman was sitting.

According to eyewitnesses, the woman was clutching the shivering infant close to her chest. But the baby was alive! Both of them were alive!

This, in a nutshell, epitomizes the meaning of commitment, of hope and faith. Despite the situation, she set out to achieve the impossible with total clarity, without looking right or left, without any ifs or buts, without the slightest shred of doubt. Her conviction was steadfast, and of course, there was always the burning desire of a mother to save her newborn. For what desire or conviction stronger than a mother's to save her child? She knew nothing else. The signals that she had sent to the Universe were tremendously strong and the Law of Attraction had taken no time to say, "Your wish is my command." It had gathered the impossible, moved Mother Nature and provided for her. As they say, the waters parted just for her and she walked right through!

Dear reader, if you could just stop for a moment and ponder over the nerve-racking, horrifying details of this incident, then you will understand the impossibility of the situation and hence the power of universal laws.

The Universe provides each time it has received signals of such undiluted strength. The Law of Attraction is absolute. It's 100 percent! It never fails.

If, at this point, you would like to say that it doesn't work for you, think again. Shift through your thought process and analyze the purity of the signals that your conscious mind generates and sends to the subconscious.

The way you tune your RAS will attract only those kinds of signals. If you are sending positive signals, you will get positive results, if the signals are negative, then so will the results be negative, and if it's a mixed bag than probably you need to be prepared for a surprise or a shock!

There was a man who prayed to God for years until God appeared before him and granted him three wishes. "What do you want, my son?" he asked.

The man replied, "I want my pockets to always jingle with the sound of money. I want to be surrounded by pretty women forever. And I always want to be amidst a hundred cars."

God said "So be it!"

The man became a bus conductor and his bag jingled with money all the time, pretty girls boarded the bus every day and since the bus drove through the city roads, he was, of course, always amidst hundred cars.

So remember to always be specific.

Don't be scatterbrained and send incorrect signals to the Universe. You might just be overwhelmed by the *tathastu* effect, obeyed by the Law of Attraction.

"I love the sound of money."

"I want to be rich."

"I want to make it big someday, get married to a nice girl, and have a house somewhere."

These statements are all so very vague. It shows that you are probably interested in a few good things but committed to none. So your signals are the weakest. The Law of Attraction said *tathastu* to whatever it could decipher.

The thought processes of successful people are never ambiguous, as is evident in their communication skills. When they speak they have a sense of surety about them. They seldom use ifs and buts, or fillers like "let's see" or "let me think." They drastically cut down on their 'hmms' and 'huhs' and clearly say what they have to say. This is because they are clear in their heads. Most, if not all, successful people are excellent orators. They ooze confidence when they speak, their voices are soothing, their pitch is well-modulated, and whatever they say all seems to be the ultimate truth in their chosen topic. This kind of confidence is only possible when you are committed to the subject, and this is reflected in your style of communication.

So be specific, be detailed, be certain, be committed, and success will be yours before you even know it. Sweep the cobwebs from your brain and be clear in your mind, for that is the communication you hold with yourself.

5

How People Become Rich

Why is it that only one percent of the Earth's total population holds the majority of the wealth of the planet? At BSR's Breaking through Learning Solutions, we dedicate a special session to 'How Rich People Think.' Do they think differently from us? Do they have a different approach or a unique attitude towards people or situations? If everything is in the mind, what do their minds consist of that's different from those of other people? What do you mean by 'rich,' and what was their version of 'rich' before they became rich?

Of course, like everyone, rich people operate in a certain frame of mind as well. From the time we are born, each and every moment leaves an imprint on our persona. That's what shapes us. That's what makes each one of us different from the other.

Like I said earlier, there is no data lost. Imagine a cupboard with separate shelves in our mind. There will be one shelf for every different aspect of our life - personal life, sexual life, health, relationships, goals, and achievements. And then there will be one for money.

Whatever we think about has all been stored in the cupboard of our minds. If, for instance, someone grow up hearing that money is the root of all evil, that it's vulgar, makes people greedy, leads them to unhappiness, is immoral, is a weak person's desire, and on and on - then that's the attitude they will have about money.

If someone has been taught to always save money for a 'rainy day' and not to waste it, that's how they will operate for the rest of their lives. They will always be saving money every chance they get, and will never be able to tune in to start earning.

If someone is told to "cut their suit according to their cloth," that limiting thought will always be at work while dealing with money.

No matter what these people do, they will never become rich. They will always struggle for that little extra which will make them comfortable. And that little extra will always be a little far away from them. Fifty thousand rupees extra is what they aspire for all their lives. Well, guess what? No matter how much they earn, they will always be short of that fifty thousand rupees. They earn to save, they avoid spending a little extra to train themselves so that they can earn more in the future. They are mostly afraid and have a mental block that prevents them from taking a calculated risk. They operate from that shelf of their cupboard where only limiting thoughts dominate.

On the other hand, people who were taught to earn money and respect it, welcome it with both their hands, aspire for more, and yet use it for the betterment of self and others believe that locking it away will not make it grow. Instead, earning it will. Somehow, they are never short of money and are never seen to be struggling for it. Money seems to come easily to them. But why?

Because rich people think differently from others. And research says that most rich people think alike. They have similar thinking patterns, and if people aspiring to become rich can copy those patterns, they too will succeed.

Your character, thoughts, and beliefs are critical to the level of your success. Your wealth can grow only to the extent you grow, your energy grows, and how you evolve as a person. You should challenge your present energy level. Your limiting thoughts should be dealt with and you should confront certain aspects of your personality so as to deal with them successfully.

- Who are you?

- How do you think?

- How self-confident are you?

- How is your relationship with others?

- Do you really want all that money?

- Can you handle it?

- How well can you handle situations and people?

- How well can you manage your physical or mental state?

- Do you really deserve to be rich?

It is vital to answer all these questions correctly in order to clear your shelf and change your cupboard. In that box, then you need to store the ones that will allow you to liberate your thought process and push you towards success.

Now, you will realize that there's more to richness than just reaching out and trying your hand at a particular business. So what do we mean by rich?

Your version of being rich, and my version, and the Universe's version might not be the same. Be specific: do you want to earn ten thousand, or a lakh, or a crore? Put your hand on your heart and say, "By the end of this year, I want to earn ten crore rupees and I am committed to doing so."

Don't bother about the how and the why. Just commit yourself, for there is hesitancy and the tendency to draw back and be ineffective until one is committed. The moment you commit yourself, providence moves too. A whole stream of events then emerges from this decision, bringing about unforeseen experiences, meetings, and material assistance that no person could have dreamt would come their way.

This is my first book, and when I thought about writing it, I didn't have the slightest inkling about how to go about getting it published. I didn't know who would publish my book. Who will do the printing? How will it reach the bookstores? Then there is the cover page to be designed, media houses to be involved, readers to be informed. I didn't know anything about what was involved. I just had this book in mind, with lots of things I wanted to share with you, and a laptop resting on my knees.

But as I started writing, I could *feel* my readers reading the book, and loving every word of it, and so I went on, night after night, punching the keys on my laptop. Words tumbled out and page after page flew by in front of me. While doing so, I spoke to friends and acquaintances about my desire, and things started happening. It seemed as if miracles were happening, as the information I required started coming in even before I searched for it.

There is a plethora of formalities to complete before a book reaches the hands of the readers and I didn't know any one of them. But you're holding this book, and it's as real for you as it is for me!

In other words, the Universe will assist you, guide you, support you, and even create miracles for you. It will bend over backwards to support you. But first, you have to make a commitment!

Have you ever wondered why your school friends, who came from a similar background, have a better life than yours? Perhaps they are more successful today and have more money than you. This is because they were more committed to it than you were. They believed in their thoughts and had faith in the power of the Universe. They were more consistent than you.

If you talk to rich and successful people and pose relevant questions to them, you will find that they have a definite thinking pattern.

- Rich people will tell you that they are the masters of their own lives. They would be completely confident when they proclaim that they would become what they want to become. No ambiguity here.

- Poor people, on the other hand, will tell you that life is predestined. It's fate. One is born with it and therefore has no control over it. They just need to surrender, accept, and fit into what destiny has in store for them.

- Rich people will show you the benefits of taking calculated monetary risks and work towards earning more. They will explain how important it is as the means to getting rich.

- Poor people will have convincing arguments about why it is foolish to take any kind of monetary risk, and that saving, not earning, money is the key to becoming rich.

- Rich people have the courage to dream big and believe in their dreams, too.

- Poor people think small. They are miserly even with their own thoughts. They feel guilty to think big, as they fear that they may be labeled as greedy or evil.

- Rich people sift through negative situations and grab opportunities. Even one is good enough.

- Poor people just see negative scenarios as enormous roadblocks between them and their goals.

- Almost all rich people admire other rich people. They attract each other like magnets. They club together, dine together, and share ideas.

- Poor people, on principle, stay away from all rich people. They can't believe that they acquired their money through fair means. For them, all rich people are dubious characters who have all the vices of the forbidden world. Poor people resent richness. Strangely, they resent other poor people as well. The instinct to resent each and every person for no particular reason is a very negative trait, and makes their minds as heavy as boulders.

- Like attracts like. Rich people are mostly found in the company of other rich and successful people. They also mingle with promising young men and women; they talk to them and listen to their new innovative ideas.

- Poor people keep their associations limited to people like themselves, too. They like to get together and talk about each other's failures and wonder why life is so unjust. And after a good meal, they go back home to brood some more.

- Rich people like to perform and base their rewards on the basis of their performance. They are not bothered about the time or the effort. They are only concerned about completing what they have set out to do. They have to get the job done successfully before they can accept a reward.

- Poor people expect to get paid after they have invested their 'valuable time,' and never mind if the work at hand is incomplete or in a mess. They have tried, they have put in the effort, and now they need to get paid.

- Rich people like to live in abundance. They work hard and play harder. It's not just the money that allows them to enjoy themselves, it's their attitude towards it. They know that they only live once, and they are ready to make the most of it. Not that having fun necessarily involves money!

- Poor people forget to live. All their energy goes into earning money and not enjoying it. They believe life is hard and that is how it is supposed to be. Only kids have fun. Adults are supposed to toil. So for them, it's not just the lack of money, it's also the lack of attitude. It doesn't cost money to sit in front of the TV and enjoy comedy shows with your loved ones. But they can't. Attitude!

- Managing the state and managing their money is the magic mantra of rich people. If they know how to make money, they definitely know how to keep it and make it grow further.

- Poor people are poor managers of money. They mismanage what little they have. Interestingly, they tend to spend money on unnecessary things because they are cheap, rather than spend it on something that is necessary but costs more. For example, they would rather invest in going for dance classes instead of investing in good computer coaching, which would probably be more useful and lucrative in the future. Understandably the computer coaching costs more, but the dance classes are unnecessary! Poor people never tend to understand this. It's strange that if these people suddenly come across money they invariably lose it!

- If you ask a rich person to tell you a secret about money, they would say, "Money attracts money."

- Ask a poor person for their secret, and they would tell say, "Work hard for money and save every paisa you can."

- The fear factor - rich people take it in their stride and march on ahead.

- Poor people overemphasize their fear and stop midway. There's no term called 'calculated risk' in their dictionary. A risk is a risk, and it's foolish to take risks. Someday when they are rich they will think about it, but today they just can't afford to. Well, guess what? For them, 'someday' never comes.

- Most rich people appreciate change. They endorse new ideas. They greatly admire the enthusiastic new generation. They are open to innovations and love new technology. They want to learn more and more.

- Most poor people are disgruntled. They are sickened by anything new and believe that the new generation will ruin the world. They hate learning anything new and believe that everything old is gold.

- Rich people have yet another trait that forms a solid foundation for their success. They love themselves. They consciously practice *self-love*.

What do I mean by self-love here? They sleep well, eat well, jog, go to the gym, and regularly groom themselves. When they dress up in front of the mirror every day, they are happy with what they see. They are super-confident about their looks. They often share the secrets of their good looks, personalities, and achievements. They are conscious of every aspect of their persona, proud of their achievements, content with their present, and sure of their future. These people have discovered from the beginning that it's very important to feel great about themselves in order to attract great things and enjoy the laurels they receive.

There was a time when I would stand in front of the mirror for hours on end and find fault with myself. I hated my dark complexion, my thin physique, my dull eyes, and the lack of 'rhythm' in my body.

I always complained. As a result, I shied away from people and had a very low self-esteem. Guess what? My wish became the Universe's command. People never found me interesting to talk to and very few people would approach me. Girls seemed to never like my company. I was jealous of those people who were bright and intelligent, who spoke with confidence, had a magnetic personality, and got special attention. This was my life back then!

When I came to the wonderful city of Pune, I was methodically made to learn how powerful and unique I am. I learnt how blessed I am to have this wonderful life. Many people aren't so lucky. I could have been born with a mental or physical defect or been born in a slum, but God chose to give me a better life. I started to be grateful about what I had. I started to appreciate myself and call myself a celebrity. I celebrated each moment of my life. Of course, the credit goes to my teachers and few friends. Today, I live every day like a king. People appreciate me for what I am doing and who I am. My presence inspires people and my talks help millions realize their dreams.

The reason I am sharing this is because until I realized my self-worth, no one valued me.

Charity begins at home. You need to start doing something first. Only then will the entire world join you. Don't expect the reverse.

Self-love sounds like an arrogant and pompous concept, but it's not. It is absolutely logical and useful. But the attitude should be right so as to not come across as arrogant or pompous. It's a surefire way to feel good, always.

And when someone always feels good, they are in a powerful field of positive energy. And being in that magical energy zone is all you need to achieve everything in life.

And another trait that rich and successful people have is the quality of communication they hold with themselves. Successful people maintain a quality of communication when they are in conversation with themselves, for the quality of communication with oneself is the quality of life we lead!

Why?

As established earlier in this book, our minds are never in a vacuum. We are constantly thinking, with over sixty thousand thoughts passing through our minds every day. Our thoughts are the modes of communication we use with ourselves. Thus we need to give our thoughts the desired direction so that they will create the required signals. By signals and results I don't just mean achievements, laurels, and accomplishments. The quality of communication with oneself also ensures our happiness, our ability to enjoy the little things in life and make every moment, big or small, a glorious moment!

Observe a toddler playing on his own and you will understand the value of ignorance and bliss and the importance of quality of communication.

When I first enrolled myself for computer classes in 1999, I was told that the basic principle that computers ran on was this:

Input - Process - Output

I was told that whatever you enter as an input will be processed and displayed as an output. Later, when I started learning and sharing about the Law of Attraction and the power of our minds, I realized that the basic mechanism of our lives is also the same. Only the right input can produce the right output.

Whenever I meet someone, I ask them, "Hey, how are you?" Almost everyone responds by saying, "I'm fine." Do you also give the same answer when someone asks you this question? If yes, have you ever thought what input you are feeding your mind? What will be the output of it? By reading this book, I know that you want to be the best, you want to achieve something great, you want to become an extraordinary person, and you really want to do something different. You want to be the director of your own life.

But my question to you is this: How will you make an extraordinary movie with ordinary input? Can you imagine what damage you are doing to yourself by using 'ordinary' words?

> *"I am a failure. I will never achieve anything in life. I will always be a failure. I am good for nothing."*

These are negative inputs you are constantly feeding yourself. What emotions do these words evoke? What images are you visualizing? Nothing good, I'm sure, and definitely not something you want to see.

> *"I am an extraordinary person who has the power to conquer my own mind! I was born to win! I believe wholeheartedly in myself. I take charge of my own life. I am an inspiration for millions and people look up to me. I am a leader and a creator. I am unstoppable! I am a shining star. I am the happiest person on the planet. I am the greatest!"*

How do you feel after reading *this* paragraph? I'm sure that right at this moment you have a broad grin on your face. Yes, that's what happens when you give yourself the right inputs. The right inputs will always help you produce the right outputs.

Now on, whenever someone asks you, "Hey, how are you?" use a more positive response. Try one of these:

- "I'm great!"

- "I'm excellent!"

- "I'm wonderful!"

- "I'm on top of the world!"

- "I'm excited!"

- "I'm superb!"

- "I'm fabulous!"

These words will condition your mind to produce the right outputs. Each word that you use has power, as it has a certain meaning attached to it. That is the reason why a wise person once said, "Speak for others what you would like to hear for yourself." That's why people say "what goes around comes around." Till this moment you were unaware of this fact but now you know about it. From now onwards using ordinary words for yourself and for others will be a crime for you, as by doing so you are putting major roadblocks in your path to success.

The thought that constantly plays in our mind is the quality of life we have or aspire to have. It can never be otherwise. You cannot aspire to lead a life that is completely different from your thoughts.

Are you constantly competing and comparing yourself with someone else? Do you spend a lot of time thinking about achieving merely to show off? Are you jealous of your friend's success or your brother's achievements? Do you constantly think ill of others? Then the quality of communication you have with yourself is very raw and uneducated. It's undignified and cheap. And if this is what you think of, then this is what you will receive from the Universe.

Improving the quality of communication with yourself will go a long way in making you a very happy person.

So now we have some very definite pointers and guidelines to becoming rich. We have also understood the concept of the quality of communication with ourselves. What do we do now? We think about those pointers and initiate a change within ourselves. We need to see which category we fall into and decode the secret behind our thinking process.

But simply knowing all these things will not suffice. They will give you a definite platform and a starting point. These things need to be implemented and to begin with, you need to be open to change. Consider each one and discard the ones you think will be detrimental to your growth. You need to always keep your mind open and be willing to try out something new.

Practicing the Law of Attraction, commanding your thought processes, and emitting positive energy to the Universe are all easier said than done. Human beings are creatures of habits. It's

difficult to break an old thought process or create
a new one. There will always be an element of
resistance. People who are committed to their
dreams break through the resistances or at the
very least try to reduce them as much as possible.
They overcome them and make a huge dent in
their old habits. They make headway.

How?

That's the power of commitment. So, do this:
stand up, place a hand on your chest and say, "I
am committed to start my business by the end of
this year," or, "I am committed to score 98 percent
in my exams," or whatever it is that you desire!

Have you done it?

…

No?

…

…

…

…Still not?

Do you think this practice is weird? If so, dear
reader, you are still not in the groove. You have
some more work to do.

Mentally labeling an idea as 'weird' or 'stupid'
is how the mind resists. Once you are committed
to your dreams, you will find that it is easy to

clear these blocks. Ego problems, stubbornness, jealousy, back-biting, unnecessary small-talk, negative talk, and talk of illnesses and disease are different examples of mental blocks. If you interact with prominent people who are successful achievers, you will realize that they never indulge in such pettiness. They have freed themselves from these poisons. They don't let such negative thoughts cloud their minds and dilute the concentration of their positive thoughts. They are all aware! The legends of the past also knew the magnetic power of the energy field. Einstein, Alexander Graham Bell, Neil Armstrong, and Aryabhata (the Indian mathematician who introduced the number 'zero' and forever changed the world of mathematics) - they all knew everything. They never thought of any act as 'weird' or 'pointless.' They allowed themselves to do a million foolish things until they made their discoveries and inventions and changed the earth. And today they are household names!

But why am I mentioning these people to you? Because before they started off to achieve something, they got rid of those mental blocks. Standing in front of the mirror and saying something is unimportant. But finding it so utterly impossible to do something so simple is a mental block. To believe that you can't do something just because you've never done it before is just a bad habit you need to break. Honestly, even if you try to do it later, when I'm not breathing down your neck and urging you to do it, you will still find it very difficult. You will be extremely uncomfortable with this 'weird' act and keep feeling awkward throughout the day. You will find it absolutely unbelievable that you have actually done something so stupid after reading a book!

This discomfort is a part of the habit of doing or not doing something. Breaking it is so uncomfortable that you quickly want to get back to your comfort zone. And that's where the power of commitment comes in. It makes you break through everything and do the impossible in order to achieve your dreams. No wish is too weird or a dream too impossible with the Universe backing you up.

Around two years ago, I was invited to a friend's house for lunch. Her elder sister, who had come for a holiday with her two children, was there as well. I was delighted to see her! It had been years since we had met. During lunch, I noticed that she was merely nibbling at her food. She was toying with her spoon and pushing her food around on her plate. I was surprised, because I knew that she had a voracious appetite and loved eating food. I asked her what had happened and asked her whether she was unwell. She laughed and replied that she was perfectly fine, but she had put on a lot of weight after her two kids and was trying to control her diet.

I interrupted her. "Who says you're fat?"

She shrugged. "Well, I can see it for myself in the mirror, and besides, everyone says so."

"Then from now on, whenever you look into the mirror, say this: 'I am thin and slim. I have the perfect body that I have always wanted and I am in perfect health.' Say this every morning when you wake up and before you go to bed. Say this before every meal. Say this whenever you are feeling low and upset about your weight. Imagine yourself with the body of your favorite film star and buy clothes that are exactly the size that you want to be."

She burst out into laughter, saying, "And waste all that money? You must be crazy! What good would imagination do?"

"Just try it," I insisted. "Try it for at least six months. Write down the exact weight that you want to have and paste it on your mirror. Buy a measuring tape and measure yourself every day. Believe in it and make room for it by buying clothes of your desired size. No matter what people say, see yourself in perfect shape and size. Eating does not make you fat, but thinking 'fat' does. Once you really start thinking about yourself as beautiful and slim, your wish will be granted." Very reluctantly, she agreed to give it a try.

But hardly two months later, I met my friend's sister again, and she was elated with the results! She said that this was the first time in her entire life that she was happy with her body! She was wearing the clothes she had always wanted to wear but never could. She said that she just could not believe that mere thoughts could make so much difference.

Some people are diagnosed with slow thyroid. Some people are told that their bodies have a slow rate of metabolism. Then there is the hereditary factor. For women, pregnancy and childbirth play a big role in increasing their body weight. These people are conditioned to think 'fat.' Once they accept and believe in any of these reasons, they start putting on weight. They then think it's a natural condition and they feel powerless. They become fatter. They start to lose hope. But to apply the Law of Attraction, that they have to start off by thinking 'thin' thoughts before they actually start losing any weight.

It is impossible to lose weight while simultaneously thinking 'fat' thoughts. It completely defies the Law of Attraction. You must feel good about yourself, about your body, your hair, your skin, your eyes, the clothes you wear, and the way you look. Every time you look into the mirror, it is imperative that you see a beautiful person in the reflection.

When I was in the eighth standard I used to go to a maths professor for private tuitions. He took tuitions in batches and we were a batch of six boys and girls. There was one girl I remember from our group because I unexpectedly ran into her just a few days ago in a restaurant. There was nothing special about her for me or anyone else to remember, except that she was the only one in our group who didn't fit in. She was an annoying person and was always on the defensive even when there was no need.

She wasn't exactly unattractive, but there was something about her that put the rest of us off. I know that it is very unfair to talk about a person in such a manner, but there is a reason for it and I want to share it with you, especially my female readers.

That day at the restaurant when she came up to me and said "Hi!" to me all of a sudden, I was surprised. I wondered how this could this be the same person. How was she looking so beautiful? She was so gorgeous that I couldn't stop myself from showering her with compliments. But what intrigued me was the way she reacted to them. Before thanking me, she said, "Yes, I know," by which she meant, "Yes, I know I am beautiful, and thank you." The style was a little unconventional. Her smile was pleasant, her face was radiant, and her eyes were now sparkling with life. I had to ask her to sit down and talk to me for some time. It wasn't just because we were old acquaintances. The change in her had been massive, and I knew that there had to be something to it.

"I live in Bangalore now," she said. "Around four years ago, I attended one of your sessions in Bangalore."

"You did?" I replied, truly surprised. "Why didn't you walk up to me after the session?"

"I had sent you several e-mails," she said with a smile.

"But I do reply to e-mails."

"You did, but you did not recognize me. But that's not the point. The point is that my life changed completely after I attended that session, and that's what I wanted to tell you in those e-mails." She gave a beautiful laugh.

I wanted to know more and asked her if she could share her story with me. She readily agreed. This is her story.

She was not a very beautiful child when she was born - small, black, shrunken, underweight, and with a head full of curly hair. For the first two years she was a sickly baby and it was a struggle to keep her alive. As she grew older, she was constantly teased for her ugly looks - good-naturedly by her cousins and unkindly by her schoolmates and friends. But she was too young to retaliate or to distinguish between who was being mean and who was being kind.

In school, she was always made to stand in the last row of the choir, and kept as an extra in the basketball team, even though she played well. At home, she felt that her mother deliberately bought her ugly clothes and refused to allow her to apply makeup because it did nothing for her.

Whenever she went out with her cousins, they rarely gave her extra time to get ready. "Wear anything," they said. "How does it matter?"

Such comments had a profound effect on her. Every time she looked into the mirror her ugly reflection stared back at her. Her clothes were always shabby, and no matter how much tried, she couldn't find a color that suited her. If someone was good to her, she always assumed that they had some ulterior motive. When someone was rude, she fought back relentlessly and without any dignity. She had always lacked self-esteem.

At school, when the teachers reprimanded her for low grades or late attendance, she felt that they were being cruel to her just because she was ugly. She never tried to be nice to anyone. What was the use? No one was nice to her. She was a total misfit in society. Life was difficult for her but there was nothing she could do about it, so she had waged a war against it. There was a battleground all around her.

She told me that after attending my session, she found so many of the things I had said were true. She could personally relate to many of the examples that I had shared at the workshop. She tried to remember what I had said. "Why don't you write a book about everything you say? Then I won't have to tax my memory. I can open the book anytime and choose what I want to read."

One thing that struck her after my session was that by hating herself so much, she had blocked all the good things coming towards her! How could anyone love her when she hated herself so much? There was nothing positive about her. All of her thoughts were negative. She believed that she had to fight for what she wanted to achieve. Nothing in this world was easy for her.

My session made her realize that life was indeed difficult for her because her own thoughts and wishes had made it so. She had defied every guideline in the rulebook of the Law of Attraction and had then expected to attract good things towards her. She then blamed destiny for her ugly looks when things did not turn out as per her wishes. What a catastrophe!

How could she look beautiful when she felt so ugly inside? How could anyone fall in love with her when she hated herself so much? How could she be happy when all her thoughts were sad? How could good things come her way when she saw only bad things all around her?

Once she got the drift of the flow of her thoughts, she was amazed when she realized what she was doing to herself. She knew she had to put a complete full stop to it and make a U-turn. She wrote down all her thoughts - both positive and negative - and analyzed them.

She vowed to herself that every time she looked into the mirror she would see someone beautiful.

She would then first stand in front of the mirror and say thank you for a perfect body - her hands, legs, eyes, lips, nose, hair, and perfect height. Her skin, she observed, was flawless, and her voice was sweet. Wow! She had never noticed this before. She made herself think that she was indeed beautiful and that the clothes which she wore were great.

With each passing day she admired herself more and more and then something happened which had never happened before. She received the first compliment of her life! Her colleague said she was looking very different today - that she was, indeed, looking beautiful! And she received many more compliments over the course of the next few days.

The world became a bit more tolerable and things started coming easily to her. She even received an invitation to a get-together at a friend's place, which never happened before. She was even asked to host the office's annual event. She was thrilled by everything that was going on around her. Suddenly life became real and she found herself surrounded by happiness.

And then one fine day, the unthinkable happened. The man of her dreams proposed to her! He was one of the most handsome guys around and also the most eligible.

She had always secretly admired him but never thought that there could be anything between them. But now that she realized she was beautiful, she had dared to make a wish. And the Universe, of course, declared, "So be it!"

And it's not just about your coveted weight and figure, or how beautiful or ugly you are, or your dream partner. Did you know that today doctors are actively researching alternative curing methods, and that one of the methods is to activate the power of the mind and thereby trigger cures? You may wonder where the science lies, however. So here it goes:

The building unit of a body is a cell. Cells in the body are replaced on a daily basis. Old cells give way to new ones. Those are the dead cells that we scrub off to look nice and fresh. Organs are made of cells as well and they keep regenerating new ones. So, going by this theory, we have a brand new organ to flaunt every few weeks! So, then, medically, if we succumb to some disease, it gets replaced from time to time.

Then why does one person die of a certain disease while another is cured? How come Yuvraj Singh, a cancer survivor, is back on the field with a renewed burst of life and vibrancy? If you look at him, you might think that he's just had the flu or that he's returned from a long holiday in the Mediterranean! He definitely doesn't look like someone who has fought cancer. We have all seen many of such patients and we all know what they look like.

What are medical miracles? How do they happen? And why don't they happen to everyone? Is it because God doesn't love everyone equally? Does God love Yuvraj Singh or Lisa Ray, who has survived terminal breast cancer, more than us? Where is the missing link?

The missing link lies in the conviction of the patients. For some weird reason, many people believe - or rather like to believe - that they are dying, even when they are simply down with the flu! They may exaggerate their illness, cough a little more, whine a little longer, and look out for sympathetic shoulders. It certainly feels good to have someone pamper you when you are unwell, but do remember that that's exactly what you are asking for from the Universe. As per the Law of Attraction, whatever you concentrate on expands. So by concentrating on your illness, in order to attract attention, you are only attracting more lethargy. As long as it is the seasonal flu, it's fine, but the 'I am not well' syndrome might attract other illnesses for which you might not be prepared!

Yuvraj Singh and Lisa Ray survived because they had conviction and faith in their full recovery. They did not waste time thinking about how terribly sick they were. Instead they constantly thought about getting back to their respective fields—Yuvraj Singh on the cricket field being cheered by his fans, and Lisa Ray looking like a diva walking down the ramp. They did the needful, went through the treatment, and said "tough luck" to their illnesses.

And the Universe responded, "You got it!"

Have you ever noticed that people who complain of bad health are almost always ailing? They always have something or the other to grumble about. On the other hand, there are some people who are never sick. Poor people, for example, never complain of illnesses, which they dread. For them, doctors and medicine equals money, which they aren't willing to spend! So they convince themselves that nothing is wrong with them.

More often than not, they prove themselves right. Poor people live to a ripe old age without paying huge medical bills year after year. They endure the atrocities of life and work hard to earn their daily bread. How do they manage to do that? They do so by conniving with the Law of Attraction to keep them in the best of health so that they can continue to work in order to sustain themselves and their families.

They avoid diseases by just being ignorant about them. They can't attract something they don't have knowledge of. The Law of Attraction says you will get what you want, not what you don't want!

Doctors usually keep a stock of a medicine called a placebo. These are nothing but sugar pills and can do no to harm the body. They are for people who like to believe that they have some problem or the other and that they cannot be cured without medicine. Doctors, especially family physicians, follow this pattern. Most headaches, backaches, and fevers are often just conjured up by the mind. They are rarely actual illnesses. When doctors realize this, they simply prescribe the placebo and the imaginary illness vanishes! Such patients believe that medicine can cure them. And so they do get cured.

Extremely busy people seldom fall ill. You will never hear them complaining about headaches, stomach aches, or fevers. They just don't have time any of those ailments. So the Law of Attraction complies with them, saying, "You got it! You create your destiny!"

Do you know that people with bad eyesight are now advised to encourage their eyes to correct themselves? To make an effort to see without any aids! You need to *believe* that there is nothing wrong with your eyes and that your eyesight is perfect. It has been observed that if there is no serious disease like glaucoma, a cataract, or an infection, sight can be corrected just by awareness and mind power.

After observing the results of the power of the mind, many doctors have said that if they could prescribe prayers in the prescription, they would do so. Medicines are effective only if the patient wills it to be. That's probably one of the reasons why the same medicine has varying degrees of effect on different patients.

Doctors use the placebo to fool the minds of patients who don't know the power of their mind. However, people who are genuinely ill, use this very power to cure themselves of life-threatening diseases. There are several stories about medical miracles and each one will affirm the power of the mind.

If you have listened to people who have had near-death experiences, then you will know what they mean by the 'tunnel' leading to death. The description they all give is one of falling down an unending tunnel of light and dark and some colors. This gives us some knowledge of how our last journey will look or feel like.

By now, we have established the power of the mind and what it can achieve with some method and lots of awareness. Most of us fear the future. Fear of the unknown, the unseen! That's how we have been conditioned since birth. We have been methodically trained to think about a secure future, but seldom did anyone tell us how to live our lives today. For that's all we have. I am reminded of a beautiful quote that goes like this: "Yesterday is history, tomorrow is a mystery, but today is a gift. That is why it is called the present."

You should live today like it is the last day of your life. To most of us, this sentiment sounds nice but is extremely impractical. We are so obsessed about the future that we end up forgetting our dreams. We work, we earn, and we live a lavish life, but most of us are still unhappy.

Through my workshop *Igniting the Spark*, I try to make people aware of the single thing that will make them happy. To help them find their individual source of happiness, because most of us search for happiness in the wrong place. We arbitrarily pick someone else's dream and try to make it our own. Like wanting to become a doctor or an engineer because it's an easy option, or because everyone does so. The power of the mind tells you that dreams are real, and that each and every realistic dream will materialize if we abide by the Law of Attraction.

So I would like to stress upon a few points to assure you that no dream is futile and no fear real. The first point I want to discuss in a little detail is the concept of burning desire, for that's where true living begins - A Burning Desire.

I have talked about it earlier in the book. We all know what it is. And I'm sure that some of you are probably thinking about your own burning desires. But how do we fuel our burning desire? This needs to be thought out consciously, or else it will remain nothing but a feeble want!

From time to time, we all want something or the other. Occasionally, we receive some of our desires. Sometimes we don't. And most of the time we're okay with that. But it is only when we consciously practice the concept of burning desire that each of these wants will be fulfilled. We first need to fuel our desires every day.

6

How to Fuel Your Desires

I truly had the desire to write this book, but it was not a burning desire as I was not able to fuel it properly to keep it burning. I thought about it several times but didn't follow it through. On December 31, 2012, I sat down to set my goals for the next year. In my diary, I wrote how excited I would be on 31 December 2013, holding my new book in my hand. In fact, I achieved my goal on November 1, 2013, and today you are reading this book. My desire has become reality.

If you want to fuel your desires, here are some powerful ways which I have been following and sharing with many. I am sure you will be most interested in this part of the book as this is where most of the people fall short.

Affirmations

Having heard this term many times, I'm sure you are wondering about its true meaning.

Simply put, affirmations are positive statements that describe a desired situation, and which are repeated many times so that they can register in the subconscious mind and bring about a positive action.

The four key aspects to ensure that affirmations are effective are attention, conviction, interest, and desire.

Imagine that you are running around a football field with your friends. They are doing ten rounds, something you have never done before, but you want to win their respect and show them that you can do it too. You start running, and at the same time, keep repeating in your mind, "I can do it, I can do it..." You not only *think*, but also *believe*, that you are going to complete those ten rounds. In reality, what you are actually doing is repeating a positive affirmation.

Many of us repeat in our minds negative words and statements about the situations and events in our lives, and consequently we create situations that are not desirable. Words and statements can bring about both good as well as harmful results. People often repeat negative statements in their minds without even being aware of what they are doing. They keep thinking and telling themselves that they can't do it, they are too lazy, they lack inner strength, or that they are going to fail. Their subconscious mind accepts these as the wholesome truth and eventually corresponding events and situations come into their life, irrespective of whether they are good or bad for them. So why not choose only positive statements?

Affirmations are to humans what commands and scripts are to computers. They program the mind in the same way in which commands program a computer. The repetition of words helps your mind focus on your goal and automatically builds corresponding mental images in the conscious mind, which go on to influence the subconscious mind, similar to how creative visualization works. The conscious mind starts this process and then the subconscious mind takes charge. By using this process intentionally, you can influence your subconscious mind and transform your habits, behavior, attitude, and reactions, and reshape your life.

Results are not always immediate. Sometimes it may require more time. Factors like focus, faith, the feelings you invest in repeating your affirmations, the strength of your desire, and the size of your goal are what determine how long it takes.

A word of caution: even if you repeat positive affirmations for a few minutes every morning but go on to think negatively for the rest of the day, the effect of the positive words is neutralized! If you want results, you need to refuse to think negatively.

It is best to repeat affirmations that are short, as they are easy to remember. One great way to ensure that you repeat affirmations often is to repeat them every time your mind is not engaged in something important, like when you're travelling in a bus or a train, waiting in a queue, going for a walk, and so on. Repeating the affirmations several times every day can help you reach your goals faster.

Being relaxed both physically and mentally strengthens the concentration. The more faith and emotion you put into your affirmations, the better and quicker your results will be. Choosing only positive words while describing what you really want is important. If you want to lose weight, don't tell yourself that you "aren't fat" or that you're "losing weight." These are negative statements and bring images to the mind of what you do not want. Instead, say that you're "becoming slim" or that you've "reached your perfect weight." Such words bring positive images to the mind.

Always use sentences in the present tense, rather than the future tense, when you affirm. Saying that you "will be successful" means that you intend to be successful someday in the future, rather than now. It is much more effective to say that you "are successful now." The subconscious mind will work overtime to make this happen in the present.

The power of affirmations can help you transform your life. By stating what you truly want in your life, you mentally and emotionally see and feel it as true, irrespective of your current circumstances, and thereby attract it into your life. Here are a few examples of positive affirmations:

- I am fit and in perfect health.
- Riches are pouring into my life.
- I am getting wealthier every day.
- My body is healthy and functioning at its best. I have abundant energy.
- I learn and comprehend information quickly.
- My mind is calm and at peace.
- I am always calm and utterly relaxed.
- My thoughts are under my control. I radiate love and happiness.
- I am living in my dream house.
- I have an amazing, loving relationship with my spouse.
- I have a wonderful, satisfying job. I am successful in all my endeavors.
- Every day, in every way, my life is getting better and better.

An Abraham-Hicks Technique

This technique says that if we can put in 17 seconds of pure undiluted thought towards the achievements of our goal three to four times in a day, we have done a great job and that we are speeding towards success. Abraham further says that 17 seconds of pure thought are equal to 2,000 action hours, 34 seconds of pure intention are as powerful as 20,000 action hours, and if this duration is increased to 68 seconds then the energy multiplies and holds the power equal to 2,00,000 action hours. You would probably be surprised to hear these numbers but it's true, as this is how certain people attract all the good things in life without even constantly working for them.

Why 17 seconds? Because that's the maximum time span we can hold an undiluted thought. Most of us cannot complete a sentence without contradicting ourselves a couple of times. And that's within less than two seconds. This sends mixed signals and our goals are pushed further away. For an example we say, "I really want this new car, but it's so expensive that it's impossible for me to afford it."

Abraham says that a pure undiluted thought holds good for 17 seconds after which it burns out and gives birth to another thought. Because this other thought is a new one, it is more powerful than the previous one which has been exhausted by now. So the new thought, by the Law of

Attraction, will have the power or a higher energy level. If, for some reason, the second thought is negative and contradictory to the first one, the first one will be nullified by it.

So now that we know it, we should have three-to-four sessions of pure thought and consciously not follow it with negative contradictory thoughts. If we can manage 34 seconds or 68 seconds a day we have done great for ourselves.

So how do we get 17 seconds of pure undiluted thought? Most of us would find it impossible to sit down and think of something for 17 seconds without our thoughts wandering. Instead, write it down, and be as detailed and articulate as possible. Create a detailed image. If your thoughts are about a new house, imagine it in detail. The living room, the bedrooms, the color of the paint, the kitchen, the sitting area, the balcony and terrace, the color and texture of the draperies, the door knobs, the bathroom faucets, the electrical attachments, which shops to visit, what furniture to choose, where to place them, and so on. Try and chalk out each and every single detail. This will occupy your entire attention and tug hard at both your conscious and subconscious mind, demanding your full attention. So here you will get your 17 seconds of pure, undiluted thought.

Harnessing the Power of Incantations

When you are angry, fearful, ecstatic, miserable, joyful - what are you doing? You are practicing incantations at those times.

You must be wondering what those are. The dictionary meaning of the word incantation is "the chanting or uttering of words purporting to have magical power." That's when your feelings, your actions, your words, your emotions, and your thoughts about a particular dream are all aligned in the same direction.

When you say a word with heartfelt feeling, action, emotions, and the proper tone, it gets the power to really attract things faster to your life, because that's the moment when all these five elements have congruency. At this time, your attraction power is at its highest. When you set out to achieve something, it is vital that you are in total control of yourself - that your body, mind, and soul are all in congruence. You should not be in their control.

And avoid having a monkey personality at all costs. When I say 'monkey personality,' I refer to people whose behavior responds to the external conditions - a person who reacts to people and situations. Irritating or worrying circumstances make them annoyed, an irksome colleague provokes them, a frustrating situation makes them angry, and failure discourages them. A compliment makes their day, but a single word of criticism ruins it. They make themselves a monkey to their surroundings. Their life is a string-puppet and the strings are in the hands of other people and everyday situations - they don't control their own lives. For such people, incantations are not easy. Chanting incantations - even for 17 seconds - needs enormous mental power, and a person with a monkey personality, whose mind is always elsewhere, finds it difficult to converge all his emotions into a single focus. Managing your state of mind means exactly that. No matter what the external environment is, you need to manage it at all costs. Getting swayed by emotions and forgetting everything else, or getting caught in the grip of anger and losing your self-control are detrimental to you and your health.

All exceptionally successful people are masters of this art. You will never hear of a famous personality who suddenly exposed their radical self to the outside world. They can always manage their mind. They are always practicing incantations and it comes to them naturally. They don't have to force themselves into it.

Feelings + Actions + Words + Emotions + Thoughts = Incantations

Feelings are the thermometers of your thoughts. Having said that, we need to understand that we have to inculcate positive thoughts to send positive signals to the Universe for positive results, and that negative thoughts are detrimental to the realization of those very dreams. We now know that we have around sixty thousand thoughts passing through our heads in a single day! Since it's impossible to monitor all of them, we consult our feelings. If you are feeling good, your flow of thoughts is definitely positive. If you are *not* feeling good, then your flow of thoughts will undoubtedly be negative. It means that you need to do something immediately to improve your mood. Tune back once again to the frequency of positive signals and then try and keep on track.

Positive feelings have the potential to trigger positive actions. Usage of positive language and emotions can also trigger happiness. When you are in the zone, you are in perfect harmony with the Universe. Your signals are at their strongest and the Universe says, "Your wish is my command!"

The Power of Visualization

Visualization has proved to be a very powerful concept and is extremely effective if we do it with great dedication.

If it's an expensive car that you desire, that you have seen on the streets these days, go ahead and visualize it. Search for information about it in the latest magazines and newspapers. Look it up on the Internet. If possible, visit the showroom and sit in the car. Take it for a test drive. Touch it. Feel it. Fantasize about it to the extent that even if you are driving your old car, it feels like you are behind the wheel of your dream car. The idea is not to get paranoid about it, but to make it a part of your everyday life. Be comfortable with it. Think about it all the time. Your wish will be granted to you.

Many people who have read about this concept have followed it up to some extent. However, most get disappointed and give it up if they don't see instant results. So here are few tips for you to follow during this process of visualization:

- The Universe doesn't have the concept of time. Time has been created by man for his own understanding of day and night, and to calculate his lifespan. You can't expect the Universe to give you your dream car or home in a day, or even in a year. The Universe responds to the frequency of your feelings and the intensity of your desire. Low-intensity feelings plus low frequency of repetition equals slower results, and the reverse also applies. Hence, don't ask the Universe how long it will take for your dreams to materialize. Instead, just keep on visualizing till you get the results. The beauty is that the more you follow your heart, the faster the manifestation will be.

- Don't just visualize for the sake of it. Enjoy the process and be joyful about this activity. Visualization should give you goosebumps. You should visualize your goal with a broad smile on your face, with your body in the position it would be in when your desire comes true. Your breathing pattern should also match the happiness you feel when your wish comes true. You can't fool your mind. If you visualize without feeling anything inside, then your mind will never agree to it. Feelings are the most important parts of your visualization. The key is that there should be no difference between your desired physical and mental states and your current physical and mental states. If your current frequency of thoughts and feelings can match your desired frequency, then the attraction will happen at a much greater speed.

- If you want something from your parents or friends, you might ask them once or twice and they might agree, but if you keep nagging them, they might get irritated and assume that you don't trust them. Everybody hates a nag. Consequently, their behavior towards you will be negative. In the same way, don't keep visualizing all throughout the day. If you do so, then you are clutching it and not letting it float through the entire Universe. This will also communicate to the Universe that you don't trust its ability. And it will slow down the entire process of manifestation. So it's best to visualize twice a day - once in the morning and once at night before you sleep. Once you have visualized it, let it go.

- Visualize out of love and don't try to control your mind while it's visualizing.

Let it flow in its own rhythm and at its own speed. Remember that the mind doesn't like force. Don't create any image forcefully. Be happy with what comes to your mind - just accept it. Just direct the flow, but don't control it. Your mind is more intelligent than what you think it is, so believe in it and its powers will be unleashed.

Stop Being So Desperate!

Some time ago, in one of my workshops, a girl asked me, "Sir, many times I want things and I work really hard for them. They are my burning desires and I do everything to turn them into a reality but it still doesn't work - why does this happen?"

She was shocked to hear my reply: "What you call your burning desire - I call it desperation."

I explained her further that when you are desperate, you are not happy and your happiness is essential for you to achieve that end result. When you are working for a goal with lots of unhappiness, then what are you attracting? You are attracting more reasons to be unhappy. That's why it either takes a very long time to materialize or it doesn't materialize at all when you are desperate for something.

Most people don't get what they want in spite of putting in lots of effort and energy. This is because they aren't happy and don't feel joy for what they are doing. They do things mechanically and are desperate for the end result. Desperation is a negative state and has a low frequency. It's like wishing to buy something for a thousand rupees when you have just fifty rupees in your pocket.

You must have observed that people rarely get the things they want when they are in dire need of it. For example, if you have left your existing job and are searching for a new one, it may be difficult for you to find another position; whereas if you search for a new job when you are already employed, you might receive several offers. Have you ever experienced this or do you know people who have? There is a very thin line between desperation and burning desire. If you are aware of this, then you will always be a magnet who can attract anything and everything.

Be happy and move smoothly towards your goals. Enjoy the process. If you are able to enjoy it, then the destination may not matter at all.

Let Go to Get More

On the occasion of Shri Krishna Janmashthami, I went to see the *dahi-handi*, an event where people make a human pyramid by climbing on top of the other to reach up and try to snatch a pot hanging high containing curd and butter. While observing the entire process, I realized that the person who was climbing up had to let go of his fear of falling. You can only climb up if you let go of what you are holding on to.

The process of manifesting accelerates only when you learn to let go. Only if you let go of your past grudges, past challenges, past programming, and past results can you move on to a higher and better future.

On one hand, you may have a burning desire but on the other, you are holding on to trivial things that will always pull you down and stop you from achieving what you are capable of. It's as if you have the desire to drive a Mercedes-Benz but you are stuck with your old Bajaj Chetak scooter.

Here are some simple yet powerful steps that can help you let go of your past and other unimportant things and also help you focus on something that is better and brighter:

- *Meditation.* It helps you find tranquility and peace. It is an action. The fact is that our bodies can be brought to a rested state much easier than our minds. This is because our lives have a much faster pace and are flooded with external noise and distractions. Clarity comes from within. Meditation is the process of reaching deep within.

- *Understanding.* Don't judge, but try to reflect upon your past as if you are an unbiased third person. Just observe! Realize that you are not your past. Understand that your experiences were created by the situation and the people in your life, and that those experiences are not you, nor did they create you. Knowing and understanding your past and some of your patterns will help you to recognize your self-destructive behavior. Understanding creates awareness, and awareness helps you break the cycle.

- *Acceptance.* Accept your past, the people who have been a part of it,you're your circumstances, and know that none of them define you. Acceptance is the first step to letting it go and setting yourself free.

- *Empty your cup.* Doing this creates space for new experiences, new achievements, and a new perspective! Deliberately and proactively work towards letting go of your experiences, your judgments, your ideals, and your material possessions as they have no 'real' value. It's a myth that they make you stronger, healthier, or more powerful! Empty your expectations of how, who, where, and what you should be as they too hold you back from 'simply being.' Once you let go, your life will be more purposeful.

- *Alignment.* Do you know what your core values, life purpose, goals, and action plan to achieve them are? If not, take a moment to reflect and jot them down. Take all the time you need. It's definitely worth it...

Done? Great! Look at your core values and recheck if they are in sync with your goals and your action plan! If the answer is a 'no,' maybe it is time to create new core beliefs, goals, or action plans? Jot down as many new actions as you would like to undertake.

- *Flexibility.* It seems ironical to be detached from outcomes when you are working towards set goals. In the right areas, flexibility is important - like willingness to let go of the result. Learn to be flexible, allow the plan to flow as it will, for in the flow many opportunities come into our lives.

- *Giving.* Past events and experiences have a tendency to hurt or upset us. When faced with such a situation, try giving - make someone else's day brighter! Smile at someone as you pass them by, open a door for someone, put a little money in the donation box for handicapped children, give food to the needy - these small acts of kindness can have a lasting impact on your life and will help you put your situation into perspective. Creating a sense of well-being for others is the best way to align with your inner self.

- *Believe in yourself.* Believe in your existence, your purpose. Believe that the Universe is unfolding as it should and that you have a divine role to play in the unfolding!

- *Love life.* Be happy. Have fun. Be a player, full of cheer and positivity. Give power to positivity. Love yourself, love others, and love your life. Life is a gift for you to unwrap each and every day, to gaze upon it with new and excited eyes.

- *Gratitude and self-integrity.* Follow the above guidelines and be grateful for the blessings in your life. And above all, be true to yourself.

Focus on Giving

Give and you shall receive. Givers always gain. You must have heard these phrases even as a child. When you give more, you receive more. When you give you can expect the unexpected.

During my tenure at Symantec, I developed a habit of meeting all the people before I sat down at my desk. I continued this ritual during my association with the organization. When I used to shake hands with everyone, I often came across a colleague of mine called Amey. Amey was a very nice guy and good with people, but I couldn't understand why he never responded to my greetings. He ignored me. Whenever I offered him my hand, he never looked at me and never smiled. I didn't like it, but I still persevered. We worked together in the same assignment for close to fourteen months but he never changed.

It was my last day in that particular department as I was being moved to another in the same organization. My office location was also being changed. On my last day, Amey walked up to me and told me that he wanted to have a word with me. Surprised, I said okay. We went out and made some small talk. All of a sudden, Amey said, "Bhupendra, I know I have never spoken to you much and never responded to you the way I should have. Do you know the reason behind it?"

I replied, "No, I don't."

He said, "The reason is because I don't like people coming from other states and taking the jobs that belong to our people. The people who come from other states make fun of us and do not respect our culture and our tradition. They don't value us the way we should be valued. Hence I am against all of them and that was the reason I was against you as well."

He continued: "But today I must say that you have won my heart. People like you are required in the state of Maharashtra. If you ever need any support, please let me know. Never, ever leave Pune. We need you, Bhupendra."

This was the most precious gift that Amey ever gave me. Even now, I don't know what I did to win his heart, except shaking his hand every day, in spite of him ignoring me. But it was this small act of shaking hands that helped me receive this big honor. This, I believe, shows the power of giving.

If you give, you will certainly receive, in one form or another. The more you give, the more you receive, as the Universe always maintains the balance. There can never be imbalance in the Universe. I would recommend the following practices which will certainly make your life better and will open doors for receiving:

- Learn to appreciate with honesty and appreciate as many people as many times as you possibly can. Avoid false appreciation. Be generous with your praise.

- Greet everyone and everything in life with a smile.

- Don't use ordinary, low-energy words while talking about others, yourself or situations. Remember, the quality of your communication determines the quality of your life.

- Offer help to people in need.

- Be calm and think before you speak.

- If you've decided to pay someone, then feel good when you do so.

- Increase the use of the three most important phrases: thank you, please, and sorry.

- Forgive and forget about the past. Move ahead.

From this moment, start appreciating people. Be the reason for their happiness. Feed a homeless person. Start giving as much as possible and you will keep becoming richer.

Make a Vision Board

In the corporate world I have often come across people who pin up their dreams on the bulletin boards at their workstations. These could be their dreams for a new car, their dream home, their next promotion, a long-forgotten hobby, a vacation, and so on. These are called vision boards. You should hang one in a place where you can see it easily and regularly. Pin up pictures of your goals. Maintain the vision board and give shape to your dreams. You don't have to spend your entire day thinking about it, but it should be in front of your eyes when you wake up in the morning and when you go to bed at night. Let it grow on you!

Due to the nature of my profession, I have had the privilege to visit different organizations and companies. When I enter any of their premises, I feel great because all their walls are painted with their goals and visual reminders about their targets. When I was working with Symantec, I remember that their customer satisfaction survey score targets were close to 80 percent, and later they increased them to 85 percent. People thought that 80 percent was a tough task, but now the company was talking about 85! We didn't find the targets realistic. But the leadership team believed in them and covered all the floors with posters and stickers with '85 percent' written on them. Surprisingly, the entire team started achieving those targets in less than three months' time.

Next year, the company raised the targets to 90 percent and it was the same story all over again, but everyone was ultimately successful in achieving it.

There are many people who come to me and tell me that after attending my workshop they prepared a vision board and they have lost count of how many of those wishes turned into reality without them constantly having to work on them. So it works!

If you are a person who has big dreams but constantly loses hope and faith, a vision board will help you focus on them. So what are you waiting for? Take a piece of chart paper at once and start pasting the images that reflect your dreams. Start creating the blueprint of your success. Don't delay it - the Universe loves speed!

The Principle of Pain and Pleasure

Besides incantations, human beings operate from a very simple concept in whatever undertaking they attempt. It's the concept of pain and pleasure. Behind every action there is this theory at work. We work towards pleasure and every pain that we go through is in anticipation of the pleasure we will receive in the near future.

This is a very powerful concept, and at BSR Sparssh Foundation, we have given it some extra mileage after studying the huge effect it has on people's lives.

A few months ago, after a session, a girl walked up to me for an autograph. Speaking in Hindi, she said that she found my session extremely motivating and inspiring. She also revealed that she had big dreams and that after listening to me, she realized that she wielded the power of fulfilling every one of them. But the biggest challenge she faced was her knowledge of English, or lack of it. To fulfill her dreams, she would need to learn the language but she didn't even know the basics.

"But after listening to you, I know I can. I definitely can," she said. "I just need to know how to go about it. It's a complex language and I am twenty-four. Will it take me another twenty-four years to read and learn this language to speak it fluently? I am trying to learn it, but finding it very difficult. After all, it's not my first language. And I have other work as well - I don't get sufficient time to invest in it."

I made her sit down then and there and list down the ten painful areas she was facing now for not knowing the language and the ten pleasures she would experience if she spoke it fluently. I also asked her to write about the pain she would have to go through in her life if she didn't learn the language in time. I told her to pause before jotting down each of the ten points and think it through, since she might exaggerate her feelings while penning it down. She was free to elaborate. I advised her to take her time.

And she did take her time! Almost an hour passed while she wrote down those twenty points. We then discussed them at length. We examined the pain she was facing for not knowing the language. We spoke at length about the mileage she imagined she would get by learning it. We also took time out to discuss the obstacles she would face while going through the learning process - time and money needed, and the difficulty of learning a new language, especially when the brain and mouth need to be trained to enunciate new sounds.

I said to her, "There will be an urge to give up, to let go and opt for an easier option. But remember that by letting go, by relieving yourself of your immediate pain, you would incur a lifetime of pain. But don't forget the pleasure you would later experience by braving this little pain."

Just over a month later, she came up to me to say thank you. To my surprise, she was not using even a single word of Hindi or Marathi to explain her thoughts. I could see that she was very confident. Yes, she made a few mistakes while speaking, but she was courageous enough to tell the world that she was learning English. I was very happy and complimented her greatly. Today, I use her story as an example in many of my sessions. She now speaks flawless English and is on the verge of realizing each one of her dreams!

How did she achieve this? The fact is that the moment her mind started calculating the pain and pleasure she would receive, her signals became automatically aligned to the job of attracting pleasure and avoiding pain. No matter how late we tend to wake up in the morning, we would never miss an important examination to be written in the morning, or miss a scheduled train or flight. Even in our sleep, our subconscious mind makes these calculations. Each and every person operates from this instinct, but most are unaware of it. Being aware of it and consciously using it to program the outcome of your life goes a long way towards achieving your desires.

If you talk to men and women who consciously keep themselves fit and look beautiful, you will realize that they not only avoid food and beverages detrimental to their health but actually hate them. They find the tantalizing aroma of a succulent piece of meat dripping with fat repulsive, and the smell of deep-fried potatoes glistening with oil puts them off. They would instead happily fork through a leafy salad for lunch or tell you how satisfying an apple or two is for dinner.

Their minds have successfully made the calculation of pain and pleasure and have aligned their signals to it. They automatically sift through things that will give them pain and are subconsciously attracted to things that give them pleasure. Human beings make this calculation unconsciously and constantly, and since they are unaware of doing so, they are also unaware of its effect. We miscalculate it for short-term benefits. We forget to consider the bigger picture and hence fail to fulfill our dreams.

I have just talked about people who have great bodies whose thought processes are aligned to the Universe. There are too many people who aspire to have a good physique who, when they become sixty, are found sitting in a rocking chair, patting their potbellies, wondering where the years have gone when they wanted to look like their favorite movie stars. They are surprised by the fact that while the movie star looks almost the same, they look old enough to be the star's father! Their 'one day' in the future never arrived.

That's because their thoughts were not congruent with their desire. They hadn't practiced incantations. Their thoughts were feeble and were not supported by the correct actions, emotions, or thoughts. They looked at the pleasure but were reluctant to go through the perceived pain. They were daunted by the temporary pain of changing their habitual diet and their daily routine of exercise. They fancied the figure of their favorite film stars, and followed their new regime for a few days with a measure of intensity and enthusiasm.

They bought new shoes and clothes, joined a gym, and woke up early to rush there. But slowly, inevitably, their enthusiasm waned. Waking up early in the morning became a nightmare, and training in the gym turned out to be too tedious. They didn't know how to make the calculation of pain and pleasure. They get bogged down by the temporary pain and keep shoving the pleasure out of sight.

That's a big miscalculation.

Don't forget that the subconscious mind still does the calculation because it's a natural process. But being unaware of it leads to such miscalculations that it overturns the total outcome. They give up, initially, muttering "it's just for a two-day break," and then the two days becomes five, then fifteen, then fifty. Eventually they forget that they even had any plan to get back into shape! Twenty years later, they still feel the pain, probably with an increased intensity because they miscalculated it.

Once when I was travelling, I got a chance to meet a man who once participated in my workshop. He was an exceptionally handsome man with an amazing personality and strong physique. I asked him what the secret to his fitness was. What he shared with me was really interesting.

He said, "Sir, there was a time when I was very thin. I was in college and I had a classmate whom I really liked. We were good friends, but I was never able to express my feelings to her. My physique was the underlying reason behind it. I used to believe that I was not at all good-looking.

Many people remarked about my thinness and joked about me looking like a bamboo cane. I wanted to work on it. I made plans to exercise so many times but I could never stick to the schedule. I even took medicines to improve my health, but nothing worked. One day, this girl whom I secretly admired passed a sarcastic comment about my figure, which hurt me a lot and made me uncomfortable. That day I left college with a lot of frustration and, to some extent, guilt welling up about my own physique. I started again with a vengeance. I began going to the gym regularly. I exercised for at least four to five hours a day, and in three months, I had a wonderful physique. People started noticing me in college, as I intentionally wore clothes that enhanced my new form, and the appreciation poured in. Since then, I exercise daily and maintain this physique."

Did you notice how one small remark from a person generated so much pain in his heart? In order to avoid that, he turned his main weakness into a strength. There are many such stories of how one slap, one insult, one sarcastic remark, one negative word, motivates someone to bring about extraordinary changes into their lives. The human mind wants to avoid pain and wants to gain a lot of pleasure! Here, this young man suffered a lot of pain when the girl he loved laughed at him, and he never wanted to go through that again. So he got motivated to turn it around.

The right calculation of pain and pleasure can

surely help in many ways, such as in:

- Making important decisions which you are unable to make, due to fear or mixed feelings.

- Eliminating procrastination and motivating yourself to take the actions which are important for you.

- Enhancing your relationships tremendously.

- Putting a full stop to your bad habits.

- Improving the overall quality of your life.

Do your pain-pleasure calculations today, especially for all those activities that can give you huge returns in life. Don't be lazy. If you learn to do the right calculations about pain and pleasure, you will certainly be very successful in motivating yourself.

Desired Value vs. Demonstrated Value

Whenever you fail to achieve something, you fail because your desired values and your demonstration of those values were very different. For example, many people walk up to me and say, "Sir, we want to become great public speakers. We really want to be able to speak confidently like you in front of a crowd."

This is their desire. I tell them that it's easy to become a public speaker - you just need to come, speak, and go back to your seat. The rest will be taken care of with time. Unsurprisingly, only one or two people out of one hundred would actually come up and speak. They don't want to sow the seeds of action but they want to reap the benefits. They don't want to take action as they are paralyzed by their fears or are caught up in their own comfort zone. You need to work for your desires to turn them into results. If your desire is to earn a lot of money, then every action of yours should demonstrate that you are money-conscious. If your desire is to be a businessman, then today is the day when you need to take your first step. Never wait until the situation becomes ideal, because that time will never come. There will never be a perfectly ideal situation. You need to act now!

Desired and demonstrated value is a very simple concept that makes your calculations easy and workable. It's like a graph that you can put up in the corner of your vision board to observe and update from time to time. When you can see your progress on the wall in the form of a graph, which is measurable, reaching your goals becomes easy.

How do you make the graph?

If you are maintaining a vision board and you have every parameter added to it, you need to put that part as the desired point in your graph. Go to your vision board and list your present status. Jot down bullet points on how much work you have done in the direction of achieving your desired object. Put that as your demonstrated value point.

Then with each step you take towards your goal draw a line higher and towards the desired value point of your graph. The climb will be fun, and since you can see it as a measurable quantity, it will be easier.

You can put in as many parameters as desired to make it more detailed - a timeline, say, or a deadline for each milestone. You can then tick them off when the job is done. As the graph lines grow longer and closer towards your goal, reaching it will be easier. The ineffectiveness will be minimized. Incantations will come easily. And achieving your desired goal will be fun.

Modeling

When we take the path to follow our hearts, we usually have a role model in our minds. It could be that we love our role model's entire personality or that we admire some aspect of it. For example, my role model is Barack Obama. I have no desire to become an American President, but I would like to have his magnetic, 'larger than life' personality. And even though I do not aspire to become a film star, I would definitely like to have Amitabh Bachchan's mastery over the language. His intonation, his voice, even the body language he adopts is hypnotic. Listening to him speak when he sits and talks to the contestants on the quiz show *Kaun Banega Crorepati* is an out-of-the-world experience. Other role models could be powerful business magnates like Laxmi Mittal or Dhirubhai Ambani, or brilliant cricketers like Sachin Tendulkar or Brian Lara.

There is a shortcut to achieving this. It's a definite and a proven scientific procedure, and it comes in very handy when we have a target personality who we want to be like. It's called modeling.

Anthony Robbins propagated the theory of neuro-linguistic programming (NLP) in a big way. He says that success leaves clues. Every trait traces a neurological pattern. If we have a role model, we need to spend time observing him - the way he walks, the way he talks, his voice modulation, his tone of speech, his approach towards situations, his attitude towards people, the way he dresses, the way he grooms himself, his likes, dislikes - you need to know everything.

By asking the right questions and by studying his behavioral patterns, you can get a map or a rough sketch of his brain. If you know NLP then it will be easier for you to obtain this. NLP is the science that helps you to understand how your brain works and how it processes the instructions, situations and commands. Different parts of the brain are responsible for a person's different characteristics. Constantly observing the person and trying to ape him means you are trying to follow his footsteps. You are tracing his neurological pattern.

By trying to copy his external features, some of

his thought processes rub in too. For example, if he wears a certain brand of shoes and you start doing the same, with time you will find that you have begun to like the brand as well, which is more than just mimicking him. Perhaps their shoes are more comfortable than the shoes you previously wore, or they match your trousers, or they have a longer life-span. Soon you will probably want the trousers or the ties that he wears. You would talk about lasagna, white wine, and which wine should be paired with which dish. So where exactly is all this leading to? You are modeling him, some of it knowingly and some unknowingly.

The more you train yourself to study the concerned person and replicate all his characteristics in yourself, the more accurate your modeling will be, and thus the closer you get to the magnitude of his success.

Anthony Robbins demonstrated this through a simple experiment on the US Army. He asked them to give him ten of their best shooters and said that he would make every other shooter like them. He applied the practice of NLP. He asked them hundreds of questions, most of which had nothing to do with shooting. He then started teaching their behavioral and thinking patterns to the other shooters. Anthony Robbins was not a shooter, so he didn't take them to the shooting range to train. He didn't even speak much about shooting. Instead he concentrated on all aspects of their personalities and made it a three-dimensional approach. At the end of the training, when they were taken to the shooting range, they were all at par with the top ten shooters. Wasn't that a miracle? No, not really! It's science. To be successful, you need a certain mindset and certain physiological traits. If you get them right, you will be successful soon. And the easiest way to be successful is to model yourself on someone who already is.

When I left my job, I didn't have a clue on how to earn money or set up my business. I dared to dream big, but I had very little money in my pocket and I was alone. All I had was a burning desire and some hope. Once, I had the chance to attend a meeting of a group called *Business Networking International*, where entrepreneurs from different genres met once a week to discuss business ideas and strategies. They exchange knowledge and are mutually helpful to one another in terms of helping them succeed in their respective fields.

When I went there for the first time, I drove up in a bike wearing jeans and a T-shirt. All the other members were wearing business suits, formal shoes, and were discussing businesses worth millions. At that point of time all I had was one lakh rupees in the bank to live on and no job. I looked on yearningly as all of them left in their expensive cars after the meeting was over.

I had to do some real hard thinking. There was a fee to be paid for the initial enrollment, there were some charges for the weekly meetings, and there was some nominal amount to be paid for the official parties that were conducted every week. Even though my situation was not favorable, I decided to be a part of this group because I knew that I would be able to extract something good from it. On top of that, I had a good amount of knowledge of NLP and hence I had trust in modeling. I started thinking about this group and finally handed over a cheque of 25,000 rupees for my enrollment. I knew it was a risk, but I also knew the power of modeling!

For the next meeting, I invested in my wardrobe and borrowed my friend's car. While on the first occasion I shied away from the discussions on lakhs and crores, this time I deliberately got involved and took initiatives. I observed each participant carefully along the lines of the NLP and tried to inculcate them in me. It did indeed make me feel different from my usual self. Initially, it felt like I was putting on an act, but slowly the act became me. I started getting comfortable with it. Earlier I wasn't sure if I could start up on my own, but after attending the meeting and interacting with all those established people, I began to think not only of being successful but also of lakhs and crores. I became comfortable with terms like 'yearly turnover,' 'sharing your best practices,' and 'monthly target.' It became less scary for me to take big business decisions where big money was involved and big thoughts, much bigger than I was capable of at that time. With time, I became accustomed to it. I practiced modeling. Today, I am where they were that day. In fact, some of them are my clients today, trying to learn ways of expanding their wealth and business.

Switchwords

Wouldn't it be great to have a magic wand that you could just wave at any situation or creative project, and have it turn out as amazing as you wish? Actually, we all have such a wand! However, most of us are unaware of it, and have never received an instruction manual for its use. Your words are your wand! Intentional creative thoughts bring about intentional desired results.

Intentional creative thoughts can take the form of images or words, or both. We can envision an image and be grateful about it like it has already materialized, or we can declare or affirm a beneficial condition or state of affairs, in words, and be grateful in the same manner. Or we can do both image and text together.

The affirmations or declarations that most people use are complete sentences, but a pioneer named James Mangan in the past century identified about a hundred specific single words that are extraordinarily effective when used as an intentional creative thought to bring about a specific desired result.

Using a single word to create with instead of a

long sentence (as in conventional affirmations or creative declarations), brings a greatly increased laser-sharp focus to your creative energy in a single moment.

James Mangan called these special words *switchwords*. A switchword is the essence of an experience, condition, or desired result expressed as a single word. Declare, affirm, chant, sing, or even just mentally 'intend' the word, and the desired result will appear just like turning on a lamp with a switch. For example, one of the most practically useful words is 'reach' - it helps you find anything you're looking for, such as:

- Misplaced items in the physical world (keys, papers, tools)

- Forgotten ideas or information in your mind or memory (names, numbers)

- Solutions to problems

Whenever you misplace something, are searching for something, or want to solve a problem, just persistently chant 'reach' either silently or out loud. Then just let yourself, and soon you will be lead to whatever you are looking for! Some aspect of your being knows where it is, and 'reach' reliably makes the connection!

Try it - it really works, and is very useful in daily life! Similarly, here are some other words you can use:

- Whenever you want to sell something, say 'give.'

- Whenever you want to make money, say 'count.'

- Whenever you want to make something beautiful, say 'curve.'

- For good health or for peace, say 'be.'

- To work miracles or for extraordinary accomplishments, say 'divine.'

There are about ninety more such switchwords for other specific purposes! Plus one master key to do anything with mastery - 'together.'

By using switchwords you can easily enjoy increased creative power, effectiveness, accomplishments, fun, prosperity, vigor of life, mastery, and life satisfaction.

You can find the entire list of switchwords on the internet. They are very powerful, so look search for them for your own benefit - these can change your entire life.

Spread Love and Joy Around

"The future, higher evolution will belong to those who live in joy, who share joy, and who spread joy." - ***Torkom Saraydarian***

Joy is the highest vibration on this planet. Everything in the Universe is composed of energy. Everything can be measured and reduced to vibrational frequencies. It's a universal law that as we think and feel, we vibrate, and as we vibrate, we attract. When we are in the joyful vibration mode, we attract what is for our greater good.

The ancient Egyptians saw joy as a sacred responsibility. They believed that when they died, the god Osiris would ask them two questions: "Did you bring joy?" and "Did you find joy?" Those who answered "yes" would continue their journey into the afterlife.

For at least the next week or so, ask yourself these two questions each and every day: "Did I bring joy? Did I find joy?"

> *"Man loves because he is Love. He seeks Joy, for he is Joy. He thirsts for God for he is composed of God and he cannot exist without Him."*
> - *Sathya Sai Baba*

Now the question is, how do you bring joy to others and always remain joyful yourself?

I don't think I need to tell you much about this because you have done this a lot when you were a kid. You just need to recall your childhood days. If you find this is difficult, then spend some time with kids and observe them carefully - you will again start developing and reusing this muscle.

Yes, become a kid once again, do everything to bring back that energy and enthusiasm. Dance and sing the way you want to, jump whenever you feel like it, laugh as loudly as possible, live in the moment, and have as much fun as possible. Don't suppress your emotions, express them instead. Let them come out. Just go with the flow. Master the art of living in the moment and joy and love will be all around.

Meditation

Meditation is a tool. It can help you combat stress, improve your physical health, reduce chronic pain, sleep better, feel happier, be more peaceful, and be present. But on a deeper level, meditation is a doorway into the unknown. It can help us get a sense of the mystery of who we are.

When you start meditating, you will notice how unruly the mind is. I remember being quite shocked by this! I noticed that my mind was all over the place. Profound thoughts about my future jostled with mundane ones about the groceries I needed. Later, I would notice that I had spent fifteen minutes running a painful memory over and over again. It was like sitting in a crazy cinema!

So, if you're starting meditation, please don't beat yourself up about your wild mind. It is a natural condition. In time, you will learn to work well with the barrage of thoughts and you will eventually find clarity and inner peace.

Here are some simple tips on how to start meditating.

- *Posture.* Whether you sit on a chair or cross-legged on the floor, make sure that your spine is upright and your head is up. If you are slumped, your mind will drift. The mind and body are intertwined. If your body is well-balanced, your mind will also become balanced with time. To straighten up, imagine that your head is touching the sky.

- *Eyes.* Try and keep your eyes open. Open eyes allow you to be more focused in the present. Just lower your eyes and let your gaze be short. If you close your eyes, you are more likely to drift away on random thoughts. However, it's more important to do what is comfortable for you. Some people find closing their eyes much more effective. It's good to experiment and see what feels best for you.

- *Focus.* In ordinary consciousness, we are rarely truly in the present. For example, sometimes we are preoccupied while driving, and then we suddenly arrive at our destination and wonder who was driving all the time!

So meditation is a wonderful way of waking up to life. Otherwise we miss most of our experiences because we are somewhere else in our minds!

Let's take a look at what focus is. In day-to-day life, we tend to equate focus with concentration.

This is equivalent to using the mind like a concentrated beam of light. But in meditation, that kind of mind isn't helpful. It's too sharp and edgy. To focus in meditation means to pay soft attention to whatever you place in your centre of awareness. I suggest using your breath as a focus. It's like a natural door that connects your inner self and the outside world. Zen master Toni Packer says, "Attention comes from nowhere. It has no cause. It belongs to no one."

Paying attention to breathing is a great way to anchor you to the present moment. Notice your breath streaming in and out. There's no need to regulate your breathing - just let it be natural. But if you have difficulty settling down, you can try counting your breath. This is an ancient meditation practice. As you breathe out, silently count one, then two, three, four, then return to one. Whenever you notice that your thoughts have strayed, simply return to one. In this way, 'one' is like coming home to the present moment. It's good to return without a backward glance.

When you notice that you are thinking, gently let your thoughts pass by returning your focus to your breath. Don't try and stop them - this will just make you feel agitated. Imagine that they are unwelcome visitors at your door, acknowledge their presence, and politely ask them to leave. Then shine the soft light of your attention on your breath.

Note that it's difficult to meditate if you are struggling with strong emotions. This is because some emotions tend to breed stories in the mind. Anger, shame, and fear, in particular, create stories that are repeated over and over again in your mind. They make us keep looking at past events. Fear looks at the future with stories that start with, "What if..."

The way to deal with strong emotions while meditating is to focus on the physical feelings that accompany the emotion. For example, it could be the tight band of fear around your chest or the boiling of anger in your stomach. Let go of the stories and refocus on your body. In this way you are honoring your emotions but not becoming entangled in them.

Silence is healing. I know that there is a lot of meditation music around, but nothing beats simple silence. Otherwise the music or sounds on the tape just drown out the chatter in your mind. When we sit in silence we actually get to experience what our mind is doing. There is steadiness and calmness that comes from sitting in silence. In time, the outer and inner silences meet and you come to rest in the moment.

Start meditating for ten minutes at a time. Only sit longer if you're comfortable and if you feel that it's too short. Don't force yourself to meditate longer if you are not ready to do that. In time, you might like to extend your meditation to twenty-five minutes. That's the length that allows you to settle your mind without causing too much stress to your body. Most importantly, shrug off any 'shoulds.' Some people enjoy sitting for an hour at a time. Others find that they can't sit longer than ten minutes. Do what feels right for you!

It's a great idea to create a special place to sit. You could even make a shrine or an altar that you can face when you sit in meditation. You might like to place a candle on your altar and objects that have a meaning for you. It's lovely to find objects for your altar as you walk. Maybe you find stones, seashells, or flowers that speak to you.

But most of all, it's important to enjoy meditation. You might like to try sitting with a smile on your face. Be kind to yourself. Start by sitting for just a little while each day. It's helpful to establish a daily habit.

Take Risks

Life is a lot like a poker game. Players put down their money and take a chance at either winning a ton of money or losing it all. There is both an element of luck and skill involved, but essentially it all comes down to what you're willing to risk. But let's go back a bit and examine the people who simply watch the game. They're not willing to take the risk involved to see what happens. And that's where the metaphor ends. You have a choice to play or not to play poker, but the game of life is different.

If life is really like a game, then the key difference

would be that you really don't have a choice whether you want to play it or not. It's one big table and everyone has a seat. So either you play it by grabbing it by the horns or allow someone else to play your hand for you. The choice is yours!

In fact, I think life and risk are synonymous with each other. Everything about life is a risk. You could be involved in an accident or fall ill at any moment. These are the everyday risks which we have gotten used to that we don't even think of them as risks!

Most people lead a mundane life. Like they have a seat at the poker table and just sit it out. But to make life better and live it with some value, risks will be involved. And the results that you will get upon taking those risks will make life worthwhile.

These risks can bring pain when they go wrong, which is why most people avoid them. But these people hardly have the courage to dream or the nerves to fulfill them. So when we talk about risks, we omit them for decency's sake. We will not disturb them. We will let them stay in their seats while the others pick up their glasses and follow life.

The five important risks in life are:

1. Caring about someone else

And why do we call this a risk? Because it can be

very emotionally taxing. If you have ever gone through a bad breakup or were forced to dissolve a friendship, you know exactly how painful it can be. But it is definitely worth the risk, because as the proverb goes, it's better to have loved and lost than to never have loved at all. Letting another person get close to you and caring about them deeply can be a scary thing. It is very simple for them to break your trust and hurt you. But the beauty of letting someone get close to you is that you get to know each other deeply and your bond together becomes tightly woven. That can be a great feeling.

2. Learning and trying new things

There's always an element of risk when you're trying something new. Starting a new activity like rock-climbing or surfing can be scary at first, but a large part of the fun involved is to overcome that fear. The same goes for life's big changes. If you want to go to grad school or move to another part of the world, you have to just jump in and do it. It's impossible to do such incredible things without expecting a little bit of risk.

3. Following your passions and dreams

How many people's dreams have been squashed before they even got off the ground? It's a sad but true statement that most people never take their dreams past the 'planning' stage. Everyone should follow their dreams, no matter how unreachable they seem at the time. I started following my dreams because of a simple thought: when else was I going to fulfill them? You can't wait for things to happen to you. And it's not as if you have another life waiting for you after you die. So the best time to pursue your dreams will always be right now.

4. Failing

The downside of taking risks is that there is always a chance of failure - otherwise they wouldn't be called risks. Of course, the thought of failure remains the biggest obstacle that stops people from taking risks, but that shouldn't stop you. I've read that big companies in the Silicon Valley often hire people who started companies that later went bankrupt rather than promoting their own people. Apparently, they admired people who had guts and who risked bankruptcy and failure. That's a good lesson for life in general.

5. Expressing your viewpoint

Everyone has a view of what's going on in the world and how things work. Expressing how you feel can be risky since you don't know how people will react. You might find some people will be hostile to your opinions. You might even find that your opinion is incorrect.

Many people are content to just sit on the sidelines and rarely stand up to share their viewpoint. But you can't be afraid of saying how you feel just because it might be unpopular or wrong. People who make the most out of their lives have unique opinions and insights. A big part of living life fully comes in being able to express those points of view.

Risks are necessary for a flourishing life. I definitely see life as a game and the risks that we take are just the stake we use to play it. And even though taking risks means that you might fail from time to time, it is better than to never take any risks at all and live life below your potential.

Besides, when you see life as a game it changes your whole attitude towards winners and losers. Games work best when even those who lose have had fun. If you thought that successful people have never failed before, think again. It might surprise you to discover that they actually have a larger number of failures than you do! Why? Probably because they took a greater number of risks than you ever did and treated each failure as a learning experience - they used it as a trampoline and bounced higher. You might as well start taking risks and see what you're capable of. Otherwise, you will just sit at the table watching life play out in front of you.

Here are the top ten ways to take positive risks in your life:

- Decide what you want, define it, and then take the biggest risk you can think of which will move you closer to your goal. Taking action towards doing what you want to do is not a risk.

- Make a step-by-step plan towards an important goal and define the risks you must take to move forward. Living a status quo life will not change any situation in which you are stuck.

- Ask yourself what's possible, not what isn't. Then make a list. Most people spend too much time pondering over things that won't work and so try to justify why taking no action is the best choice.

- Take action. Do something off the beaten track to create movement towards a goal that is important to you. Automatically, all that is unnecessary and no longer fits will crumble.

- Only strive to accomplish a few really important things each day. Life isn't about making progress, not having the biggest to-do list.

- Work to develop the relationships that matter to you. Don't be afraid to terminate the relationships that no longer work for you, and don't hesitate to pursue new ones which nourish you.

- Redefine yourself by who you are, not by what you do. Job titles are for the human resources department.

- Define and live your perfect work day. Recreate a life which works better for you versus one which works better for someone else who really doesn't care about your welfare.

- Be your own best friend. This is easier said than done, since most people tend to be their own worst critics.

- Give yourself permission to take risks in life. Otherwise, you will wait a very long time and then later wonder why change took so long, or worse still, why nothing changed at all.

Taking risks towards what you want in your life is very relevant. What might seem like a big risk to one person might not seem like much of a risk to another. Happiness in life, work, and relationships comes from the knowledge that you were not afraid to try something new in your life when the status quo was no longer in your favor. Take a few risks towards what you want - your life will be richer for it.

Find Your Divine Stone and Plant a Tree

This method truly helps you on your way to success. Get up early one day go out for a walk. Be on the lookout for a smooth, attractive stone or pebble. It should be small enough to fit into your fist, but not smaller than that. Once you've picked your stone, look at it intensely to give it power. If you would rather follow a ritual, take the stone and touch it to the idol of your chosen God. You can do it, but you need to believe in it and its power. Make the stone yours.

Now every time you face a hurdle, hold the stone tight in your closed fist and feel its divine power seeping into you. Believe that it gives you the power to solve all problems. Energize it so much that it becomes all-powerful. If you can, gather together all your power and put it into the stone. This will give you strength in a crisis. Every time you make a resolution or do perform incantations, hold the stone in your fist and feel it. It will help you focus. All your attention will be pinned onto that stone. So every time you touch the stone it will activate you and bring you closer to the realization of your dream.

Another method is to plant a tree and water it every day. Let's call it your wish tree. While planting the tree, place a silver coin at the bottom of the pot. It attracts positive energy and will give a significant boost to your positive signals as well as boost your fortune.

As you watch your tree grow, so will your fortune. But if the tree dies, don't take it as a negative signal. It means nothing. Just go and get yourself another sapling and this time try and take better care of it. Don't just leave it in the sun to dry up and die. Observe it every day. Spend a few minutes with it every day and concentrate on its growth - its tender branches, lush green foliage, delicate new leaves... feel the life flowing through it. It's better to do this in morning as soon as you wake up. It will give momentum to your fortune.

The Script of Your Life

This is a process that scriptwriters use to jot down the storyline of a movie. Follow these five steps:

- *The purpose of your life.* Why do you want to make your film? What will be its mood? Its genre? Will it be a light-hearted comedy or a serious drama with an underlying message? A tragedy or a dreamy love story? What is the purpose of this film, or let's say the purpose of your life?

- *A one-liner.* This is one line without any full stops. This line compresses your entire life into one sentence. How you would like to perceive your life? How would you want people and your loved ones to remember you? What is the one thing that makes you happy?

- *A rough sketch.* Here you will jot down roughly how you would want the various aspects of your life to look like. For example: your love for painting, your master's degree from business school, your career in training, your first painting exhibition, your first car, your new three-bedroom apartment in the suburbs, your marriage, your honeymoon in Paris, your world tour, your first deep-sea diving trip, and so on.

- *Details.* Pick up each and every pointer in your sketch and elaborate on it with great detail - which business school you want to graduate from, the make and model of your car, how you want the man or woman of your dreams to be - you get the idea.

- *Conclusion.* It could be your retirement plan, a new venture, or maybe something very different from what you've been doing so far.

The third point - making a life sketch - is a very important exercise because the more accurate you are in jotting down your aspirations, the more you will be able to keep yourself on track. Your vision board will look all the more promising, colorful, and vibrant. For the details of your life, feel free to use as many pages as you like for every aspect, from to the color of the bathroom tiles, to the names of your children, the organization that specializes in deep-sea diving, and the best hotels in Paris for honeymooners.

Don't let the government or your organization decide your retirement plan. Do it yourself instead. After all, you have lived your full quota of a life filled with action, you have fulfilled your dreams and aspirations, and now you want to take a break. You might perhaps devote all your time to a long-forgotten hobby, pick up a new one for fun, or relive your childhood through your grandchildren! Like a movie script or the ending of a movie, let it be nice and beautiful. Plan your last phase magnificently. Give people a reason to smile when they think of you.

When writing your script, avoid the usage of negative words and expressions, and always write in the present tense - never the past or future tense!

Everything happens in the present, so you must write it down as if it has already become a reality. Steer clear of negative phrases. Instead of saying, "I don't want to stay in India and work in Gurgaon," say, "I want to stay in the UK and work in London."

Here's an example of a great script that was written by one of my colleagues:

> *Woo-hoo! I'm leading an absolutely incredible life! I am the happiest, greatest, and the best. I get everything very easily in life and I am able to enjoy every moment of it. Life is beautiful. It's colorful and full of happiness, and I'm loving it! I am now the CEO of a company, and under my supervision, the company is making progress by leaps and bounds. I have received several awards,*

including CEO of the Year, Most Innovative CEO, and Leader of the Century. People look up to me with great respect and admiration. I am very handsome and people admire my wonderful physique. I visit the gym and I exercise regularly. I am full of energy and celebrate every moment of my life.

That's a fantastic script, and a good example of how yours should be. A few pointers to remember:

- The script should be full of life. It should evoke the emotions and feelings that you were filled with when imagining your new life.

- Imagine that you have already achieved everything you want and are writing the story post your achievements. Don't write about the process of achieving the things - let the Universe decide the process. It knows better than you.

Record Your Script

After you have finished writing your script, the next step will be to read it with feelings and emotions and record it. Recording it is important because you have to now let it play throughout the night while you sleep. This is the next step in the process.

The reason is because while you are asleep, your conscious mind is asleep as well. But the beauty is that your subconscious mind never sleeps. When this recording is played all through the night, it directly programs your subconscious mind for greater success, as it is not bound by those filters which the conscious mind applies before the things enter into the subconscious. This is the reason why I always recommend this activity as one of the most powerful ones. It has the power to shift your entire life, and quickly, too!

Let me tell you a story. My parents and I had been searching for a good match for my sister for the last five years. We were all unhappy and exhausted, and did not know what to do. One fine day, when I telephoned my parents, they sounded deeply worried and anxious. I was in Pune, around 1,300 kilometers away from them. I felt very sad. I cried, and when I got tired of crying, I went off to sleep.

The next morning, when I woke up, I decided to take charge of the situation. The first thing I did that day was to write my script. I wrote about all the things that I would do on my sister's wedding day. I wrote the story as if she was getting married right in front of my eyes. I recorded it and kept it playing throughout the whole night. Nothing significant happened for the next fourteen days, but on the fifteenth day, I witnessed a miracle. I found an eligible match on a matrimonial website and asked my father to check it out. To his delight, he found that the person was very suitable and was a great match. Now it was their turn to visit us and meet my sister. I again wrote a script well in advance about what would happen when they came and how they would react after meeting my sister. Happily, everything went exactly according to my script, and today, my sister is happily married to him - just as I had visualized in my script.

Even now, I am surprised by how the situation changed in less than fifteen days. I don't deny the fact that it could have been a coincidence. Some may even call it destiny. But here is a question for you: why and how did destiny suddenly become favorable when I wrote the script? Why not before? Why didn't things change overnight in the areas that I didn't write about in my script?

I understood that when the subconscious mind is well programmed then everything would go off well. This is why it's said that 70 percent of a child's programming takes place until the age of seven as until that time the conscious mind is not fully developed, and things are getting recorded in the subconscious mind.

It's just a one-time effort, and if you follow it you can get huge benefits. It's a simple three-step process:

- Write your script with passion and emotion.

- Record it.

- Let it play throughout the night, every night.

I follow this process for almost everything, and guess what? I'm living the life which I planned out for myself and which I always dreamt of.

So what are you waiting for? Close the book and write your script. Write it with a lot of positive phrases, write it with conviction, write it in present tense, and make it fun to listen to, if possible.

7

Act Now!

It's good to know the rules of life and the shortcuts that society has laid down to lead a nice and preferably easy life. However, people who are remembered today are remembered because they broke through the armor of the so-called conventional life and etched a path of their own.

So live well and don't strangle your imagination. Remember that your beautiful dreams and imagination make the world.

> *"I am enough of an artist to draw freely upon my imagination. Imagination is more important than knowledge. Knowledge is limited. Imagination encircles the world." - **Albert Einstein***

The matter I have shared over the course of this book is enough to make you aware of the immense power of the mind and its unique features. Mind power is a vast subject and inexhaustible. But since the day I started writing the book, I found it difficult to stop. *Igniting the Spark*, however, stops here. Throughout this book I have shared with you the core of my signature program.

I started my life with this program, got hooked onto it, and couldn't stop the miracles that it created. So there will be more to come, and that's a promise. This book is just the beginning of a great journey. I have had a wonderful time writing it and I'm sure that you have had a great time as well through this extraordinary journey.

So if this book has motivated you to go on a deeper, more intense, and meaningful celestial trip of the mind, tighten your seatbelts and cruise through. And what is the luggage that you will carry on this bizarre trip? Your truth! Pure intention! Undiluted attention and your honesty! Remember, the Universe only grants wishes to those people who connect with it honestly, because there is no way one can cheat nature.

Any new ideas, knowledge, or awareness is absolutely great... and also absolutely *useless*, if not put to good use. It's like we all know that if we go to the gym and exercise and follow a healthy diet, we will have a great body. But simply knowing is not good enough. Slouching on a beanbag in front of the TV with a bowl of chips and a bulging stomach will not help you achieve that great body, even with all the knowledge you have. But going out and doing the needful will help!

So knowing the power of your mind is great, but then ignoring this knowledge after you finish reading the book will not help. You have to work out your mind, just like you would any muscle. The exercises mentioned in this book have been skillfully designed by experts and proven to strengthen your mind.

Someone once rightly said that if you keep doing the same things that you have always done, then you will keep getting the same results you always have, or perhaps even less. I'm sure you have been getting the results so far, but wouldn't it excite you if you could achieve a few more things within the same time span, the same resources, and with minimal effort? I'm sure it would.

Most of the techniques that I have shared in this book won't cost money or take too much time or effort. You might dislike some of the activities or not believe in some. My advice is that regardless of whether you believe in them or not, there can be no harm in giving it a shot. From my experience of dealing with thousands of people, I can say with confidence that each technique has the power to bring about a revolution in your whole life. Act wisely.

You have got only one life. There is only one person who is standing between you and your success, and that is you yourself. Learn to part from your old ways and then you will see the treasures that life will offer you, treasures that you would never have imagined for yourself.

So fly high in the sky, go with the flow, play the game which excites you the most, take the decisions which are long pending, accept the challenges which previously scared you, dare to take the leaps which you avoided earlier, sing the song you always wanted to sing, dance the way you want, ask for forgiveness from those you hurt, appreciate those who deserve appreciation, and most of all, love yourself.

Shatter the barriers which you have created around yourself. Break free from all the limitations that you have set for yourself. Think big. Take massive leaps of faith. If you do so, you will see that the entire world is with you. Today is the day. Live it to the fullest, for you will never know whether tomorrow will come or not.

You, and only you, can take yourself to the top. No one else. You are the god and the god is you. You are the Universe and the Universe is you. Recognize that power. Honor that strength. Create a masterpiece out of yourself.

Live your life with love, passion, and excitement, and enjoy every moment of your life. I wish you all the very best! May you succeed in all your endeavors!

About the Author

Mr. Bhupendra Singh Rathore is an effective, highly inspiring motivational speaker, corporate trainer, and business coach based in India. Bhupendra's goal is to help people achieve their personal and career goals faster and easier than they ever imagined. He has been awarded Asia's Greatest Leader 2017 and Business Mentor of the Year 2018 Award.

He has consulted and trained more than 5,000 MNCs, MSEs, and SMEs, and has addressed more than 3,50,000 people in over 1,500 talks and seminars throughout the country. As a keynote speaker and seminar leader, he addresses more than 25,000 people each year.

Bhupendra addresses corporates on the subjects of personal and professional development, including motivation, leadership, business, selling, self-esteem, goals, strategy, creativity, and success.